In her excellent book *Seven Words You Never Want to Hear*, author Denise Wilson does a superb job of explaining what it means to be a real Christian. Biblically sound and understandable, it is the best book on the subject I have ever read. I highly recommend it.

AUBREY McGANN, PH.D. TH.D.,
Bible teacher, evangelist, and pastor,
author of *Saved, Sure and Secure*

With heaven-bent heart, Denise Wilson accurately and urgently unpacks these weightiest "seven words," balancing grace and truth in a way imitative of the very One who spoke them. Please! Put a Bible and this book in the hands of every precious loved one in your life…before it's too late.

CORY McKENNA,
founding president of The Cross Current

Denise Wilson states in the beginning of her book that she writes with love and a sense of urgency, and indeed she does. The breadth of her many quotations from relevant Scripture passages and persuasive quotes from prominent biblical scholars is very convincing. This book is a much needed corrective to faulty thinking of many professing believers.

GORDON RUMFORD, L.Th., H.B.A., M.A.

SEVEN WORDS YOU NEVER WANT TO HEAR

SEVEN WORDS YOU NEVER WANT TO HEAR

How to Be Sure You Won't

DENISE WILSON

Published by Redemption Press, PO Box 427, Enumclaw, WA 98022.

Toll-Free (844) 2REDEEM (273-3336)

Redemption Press is honored to present this title in partnership with the author. The views expressed or implied in this work are those of the author. Redemption Press provides our imprint seal representing design excellence, creative content, and high-quality production.

ISBN: 978-1-64645-028-2 (Paperback)
978-1-64645-029-9 (ePub)
978-1-64645-030-5 (Mobi)

Library of Congress Control Number: 2020919216

Dedicated to each person who takes the time to read this book.
I am not the same person who began writing four years ago.
I pray you will not be the same after reading it.

Contents

Acknowledgments xi

Introduction: So Much at Stake 1

1. The Christian Home Syndrome 3

2. How Jesus Evangelized 11

3. Follow Me 25

4. Examine Your Beliefs 33

5. Repentance—the Missing Note 39

6. Strange Fruit 47

7. Confession 55

8. Forgiveness 65

9. Examine Your Obedience 75

10. Examine Your Loves 85

11. Dying to Self 97

12. Those Who Counted the Cost 105

13. The Gospel of Greed 115

14. The Gospel of Self 125

15. The Gospel of Rome 139

16. Light versus Darkness 155

17. The Mystery of Salvation 161

18. The Wrath of God 171

19. The Great Reveal 181

20. The Gospel Changes Everything 191

21. Nothing but the Truth 205

Afterword: "Flee from the Wrath to Come"
(by Charles H. Spurgeon) 213

Notes 233

Acknowledgments

The first people I want to acknowledge are my mum and dad, who introduced me to Jesus as a child. In early 2015, my father went to be with his Savior. Just over a week before he died, the family was in his hospital room when he suddenly became unresponsive. We all thought it was the end, but then he woke up. When asked, "How do you feel?" he responded with one word: "Unworthy." Such are we all.

My mother has been my biggest cheerleader throughout my life. She has supported and encouraged me in so many projects, most of them started and never completed. I've finally finished what I started. Her advice has always been invaluable to me, and I've felt her love in so many tangible ways. Not only did she encourage me, but she also read through each version of my manuscript, offering helpful advice at every stage.

I thank my husband, Brad, who continually encouraged me as I wrote this book. Although a book can sit on his nightstand for a year and still be only half completed, he managed to pick up the pace and finish my manuscript in record time. He's always looking for opportunities to lighten my load, which has enabled me the freedom to write.

My sons, George and Josiah, have shown great understanding during this past year, especially as my time has been divided. They're amazing.

Brenda Thrower rescued our homeschool by pitching

in; what a blessing she has been. Josiah has been spoiled with way more stories than I ever read to him. I may have lost my job as a homeschool mom.

Sincere thanks to my friends Janet Boden, Amy Mazzuca, Loretta Tolly, and Jono Hamer-Wilson. When I clicked "send" on the computer with my earliest chapters, I felt like I was handing them a piece of my heart. They kindly and honestly offered feedback.

Thanks to Gregory Benoit and Gordon Rumford for reading through a later manuscript and offering theological advice.

Thanks to the team at Redemption Press, Athena Dean Holtz, Dori Harrell, and Libby Gontarz. A special thank you to my editor Inger Logelin who patiently guided me through my initial edit. She taught me so much.

At the eleventh hour, I was blessed with feedback from George Slater, Jim Fishback and Irene Veenstra. Their insights, combined with earlier comments from Fred Dyke, helped me to provide clarity in a few spots where it was missing.

My final editor Thomas Womack, also deserves a special thank you for refining my manuscript. His input has been invaluable.

I am so grateful for each person who has contributed their time and expertise to make this book into what you now hold in your hands.

Thank you to those who have allowed me to tell their stories.

Thanks to each friend who has encouraged me to persevere on this project. I will not name names, but I'm thankful for each of you. Your encouragement has been received with gratitude.

Finally, I thank the Lord for laying on my heart the desire to write this book and giving me the stamina to complete it.

To God be the glory.

So Much at Stake

A fter receiving a Bible from a Christian businessman
following a show, magician and atheist Penn Jillette
of Penn & Teller aired a podcast entitled "A Gift of a
Bible." In it, he said,

> If you believe that there's a heaven and a hell,
> and people could be going to hell, or not getting
> eternal life, or whatever, and you think that it's
> not really worth telling them this because it
> would make it socially awkward…how much
> do you have to hate somebody to believe that
> everlasting life is possible and not tell them
> that? I mean, if I believed beyond the shadow
> of a doubt that a truck was coming at you, and
> you didn't believe it—as that truck was bearing
> down on you there's a certain point where I
> tackle you. And this is *more important* than that.[1]

Is it possible that there's a truck bearing down on you or on
someone you love, and you or they don't realize it?

It can be socially awkward to raise that kind of question
with someone who's a professing Christian, but Jesus said,
"Not everyone who says to me, 'Lord, Lord,' will enter the
kingdom of heaven" (Matt. 7:21). There will be those who
are surprised to hear those seven words you never want
to hear: "I never knew you; depart from me" (Matt. 7:23).

Amy Carmichael wrote about "a false suavity" that

holds us back. "We are so afraid to offend, so afraid of stark truth that we write delicately, not honestly."[2]

The great burden of my heart is that you or your loved ones not be on the receiving end of those terrible seven words. It's easy to live as if there's always going to be another day, yet one day this life will be over for each of us. I want heaven to be packed with my friends, your friends, and you.

The Bible gives us many tests that can be used to determine if a profession of faith is real. Paul said, "Examine yourselves, to see whether you are in the faith. Test yourselves. Or do you not realize this about yourselves, that Jesus Christ is in you?—unless indeed you fail to meet the test!" (2 Cor. 13:5). Since God's Word is the final authority, we'll go through a series of scriptural tests to determine what true faith looks like. I'll also share stories of people whose lives have been transformed by the gospel.

My greatest desire in writing this book has been that it would be a true reflection of the heart of God for the glory of God. It has been written in love and with a sense of urgency. There's so much at stake. Don't wait until death to find out if you got it right.

Denise Wilson

CHAPTER ONE

The Christian Home Syndrome

Not everyone who says to me, "Lord, Lord,"
will enter the kingdom of heaven.
Matthew 7:21

The sermon ended, and the preacher closed with these words: "All you have to do is pray this simple prayer, and your name will be written in the Lamb's Book of Life." Then he led in a variation of the sinner's prayer:

> Dear Lord, I know that I am a sinner, and I ask for your forgiveness. I believe you died for my sins and rose from the dead. I turn from my sins and invite you to come into my heart and life. I want to trust and follow you as my Lord and Savior. In your name, amen.

Most children who grow up in the church (as I did) are given multiple opportunities to pray similar prayers. Often the invitation to ask Jesus into your heart is prefaced with, "Do you want to go to heaven?"

Who doesn't want to go to heaven? Most children, when encouraged to repeat back words that are parroted to them, will comply. I've lost count of the number of times I prayed the sinner's prayer as a child. After a while, I recall I would end my prayer with these words: "This time, I really mean it!"

Perhaps you can relate.

Despite repeating all those prayers, I believe I wasn't truly born again until I was fourteen. It happened while I was attending youth camp at Camp Medeba, a Christian camp in Haliburton, Ontario. It was then that I realized I needed to make a choice, and I decided to follow Christ. My memories are unclear as to the when and how. I just know I've always looked back on that summer as the beginning of my relationship with Jesus. I remember no specific prayer or date, but I do know my life began to change.

Before this, I was a somewhat typical church kid. I had lots of Bible knowledge, knew the "way of salvation," and had a fairly clean facade. But after camp that summer, a strong desire developed in me to please the Lord and to share him with others. My beliefs slipped down from my head to my heart and became personal. It wasn't just that "all have sinned," but that *I* had sinned. Jesus didn't just die for the world; he died for me. I needed saving, and I embraced Jesus as my Savior and Lord.

It's easy to assume that good kids from Christian homes are saved, since many of them know all the right words to say and many live moral lives. But as my father used to say, "God doesn't have any grandchildren." Everyone must come to God on their own. My parents' faith could never save me.

The Boy Who Couldn't Get Saved

The following true story first came to me via my mother, who lives in Northern Ireland. Simon and his father later wrote out their testimonies and sent them to me.

Simon was born in Northern Ireland to a loving Christian family who taught him from an early age to love the Lord and to follow him. He was that kid who always knew the answers in Sunday school. Whenever an invitation was given to accept Christ, Simon was sure to respond, since he was never sure his previous prayers had worked.

He remembers telling his friend Andrew, on the playground in primary school, how he needed to accept Christ as Lord and Savior.

In the seventh grade, he drew a line on a piece of paper. That line represented salvation. Despite having previously prayed to accept Jesus, he knew he was on the wrong side of that line.

He sometimes tried to make himself feel emotional in church because he'd heard testimonies of people crying and falling on their knees and accepting Christ. Simon tried to muster up those feelings, but they wouldn't come, so he concluded that it just wasn't the right time.

One day when he was twelve, after praying the prayer yet again, he hoped it was real this time and decided to tell his parents he'd become a Christian, knowing it would make them happy. He'd done everything the preacher said to do, and he hoped there would be a change in his life.

As he entered high school, it soon became apparent that nothing had changed in Simon's life. He'd heard how God works in the life of a believer, but he didn't see that as a reality in his life. He had no desire to further his relationship with the Lord.

At this point Simon genuinely concluded that he wasn't saved. He'd tried everything—saying the exact words the preacher said, working up tears—yet he felt no change in his life. He felt hopeless and empty.

He began to indulge in sin with little or no effect on his conscience. As he sat in the back of the church one evening, he felt resentment toward the narrow-minded Christians around him. Shaking his head, he thought, *These people are so blind*. He didn't realize it was he who was blind.

Simon loved the world—popularity, girls, and success—and he was leading a double life. His family and those in the church saw him active in church activities and Bible studies. He gave them no reason to question his salvation.

During his final year of high school, he seemed to have the ideal life. He had a girlfriend and had been accepted into four different universities to study medicine. Yet inside, he'd never felt emptier or more alone.

His girlfriend at the time was a Christian. One day Simon reluctantly went with her to a Christian concert. Between one of the songs at the concert, a band member said, "Before the throne of God, you will stand."

Simon couldn't get those words out of his head. He knew they were true and that someday he would stand before God and give account. He went home feeling very emotional and went straight to bed. The phrase *Just believe and receive* kept going through his mind.

For the first time in his life, Simon didn't have to muster up the emotion. Genuine conviction came upon him. In simple faith, he repented of his sins and was born again.

This time he knew his salvation was real! The proof was that he began to hate sin and pursue righteousness.

At first, Simon kept his salvation to himself, since his family thought he was already saved.

In September 2016, he started medical school at

Queen's University in Belfast. On Friday afternoons, after his week of classes ended, Simon's father would pick him up to take him home for the weekend. During those car rides, Simon's dad began to notice a change in Simon's personality, demeanor, and conversation. On one of those Friday afternoons, Simon's father remarked, "Simon, you've changed."

His sister was in the car, so Simon just smiled and said, "Dad, I'll tell you about it another time."

That time finally came several weeks later, when Simon and his dad were alone in the car. Simon's dad turned to him and said, "Son, you were going to explain how this change in your life has come about."

Simon was silent for a bit as he searched for words to tell what had happened. He wondered whether his dad would be disappointed in him for having lived a lie for so long. When Simon finally got the words out, he explained that he'd been saved some five months earlier.

Rather than being disappointed, his father had nothing but thankfulness to God for his mercy and grace toward his son. He realized his son had been in danger all those years without knowing it.

Before that year was out, Simon was baptized, publicly professing his faith in the Lord.

How easy it is for kids growing up in Christian homes to have heads full of knowledge and hearts that have never been transformed by the Holy Spirit.

The sinner's prayer is the most common method today for leading a person to Christ. Many look back on that prayer as the time they gave their life to Jesus. But is every child or adult who has prayed the sinner's prayer actually saved?

I would contend that no one is saved by praying the sinner's prayer. Before you protest too loudly, let me explain. It's not the prayer that saves, although someone praying the prayer may get saved.

King David said, "Let the words of my mouth and the meditation of my heart be acceptable in your sight, O Lord, my rock and my redeemer" (Ps. 19:14). The words of our mouth should echo what's going on in our hearts, but that isn't always the case.

When someone has repeated the sinner's prayer, the person sharing the gospel with them will sometimes add this qualifier: "If you were sincere, then your sins are forgiven, and you are on your way to heaven." On the surface, that sounds like a reasonable thing to tell a person, but since when has sincerity been a determiner of truth? The world is filled with sincere people, many of them sincerely wrong or deceived. "The heart is deceitful above all things, and desperately sick; who can understand it?" (Jer. 17:9). Feelings can't always be trusted in an emotionally charged moment.

You may be thinking, *But I was saved while repeating a sinner's prayer.* That may well be, but it was despite the prayer, not because of the prayer. No one has ever been saved, or ever will be saved, apart from the conviction of sin, repentance, and true faith in the person and work of the Lord Jesus Christ.

In 2009, Paul Washer preached a message called "Examine Yourself" in which he said,

> I have found that there is something quite
> amazing among parents—that if they can get
> some sort of a claim out of their children that
> they profess faith in Jesus Christ, they seem to
> hold on to that, and it gives them assurance
> and joy, and it seems that they're bothered any
> time someone would come and question that
> claim. It seems we would rather hold on to a
> false hope than to hear the truth.[1]

A friend told me recently how her well-meaning mother-in-law had written a letter to the family, expressing her concern for the salvation of the grandkids. While deeply concerned for the spiritual state of the grandkids, she also mentioned how she didn't need to worry about her own adult children since they had made professions of faith as children. Some of them show no fruit of true conversion in their lives, yet their earlier profession gave her peace.

Too much emphasis today is on a prayer, and not enough emphasis on our lifestyles. While we aren't saved by our works, how we live is an indicator of true spiritual life.

Nowhere in Scripture do we find examples of people coming to Christ by praying a sinner's prayer. I believe this method of evangelism is partially responsible for an epidemic in our churches. So many believe themselves to be saved based on a prayer they spoke. If all you have to do is repeat some simple words, then why did Jesus tell us that entering the kingdom of God is hard and that the road is narrow and there are few who find it? (Mark 10:23; Matt. 7:14).

REMEMBER

We aren't saved by repeating a prayer. No one has ever been saved, or ever will be saved, apart from the conviction of sin, repentance, and true faith in the person and work of the Lord Jesus Christ.

Ask Yourself

1. What elements of a prayer to accept Christ do you think are essential?

2. If you prayed a prayer to accept Christ, did your life change afterward?

3. How did your life change after you professed faith?

4. Think about 2 Corinthians 5:17: "If anyone is in Christ, he is a new creation. The old has passed away; behold, the new has come." Does this describe your experience?

5. Do you believe that how we live is an indicator of true spiritual life? If so, why?

CHAPTER TWO

How Jesus Evangelized

For the Son of Man came to seek and to save the lost.
Luke 19:10

If a rote prayer is not the way to salvation, what is?

Let's look at how Jesus communicated the hope of eternal life. Jesus never asked anyone to pray a prayer to prove their commitment to him. He also never used a cookie-cutter formula when sharing the gospel. He spoke one way to the woman at the well in Samaria, another way to Nicodemus, and yet another way to the rich young ruler.

While there's only one gospel, the hindrances that keep people from embracing it are not the same for everyone, which is why Jesus used different approaches.

In each of the following encounters, Jesus addresses real people who have real issues that have the potential to keep them from a relationship with him. In the same way, each of us has things in our lives that can keep us from Jesus.

A Challenge to Lifestyle: The Samaritan Woman (John 4:1-43)

The first thing we see in the account of Jesus and the Samaritan woman is that Jesus had to go through Samaria. But why? Most Jews during this period would have traveled miles out of their way to avoid going through Samaria, since Jews refused to have anything to do with Samaritans. Jesus wasn't like most Jews. He never let society dictate how he should behave and who he should associate with.

Jesus had to go through Samaria because he had a divine appointment there with a woman by a well in Sychar. This was no chance encounter; Jesus sought the woman out.

We all experience occasional encounters that we may call coincidences. I was recently struck by God's control over these things when I unexpectedly ran into some acquaintances I hadn't seen for some time. I was entering a restaurant while they were leaving, and the thought struck me that if I'd arrived even ten seconds later, we would have missed one another. What an incredible job God has in planning all these things we call coincidences.

Jesus had an appointment in Sychar at noon by Jacob's well. He had to go through Samaria to keep his appointment with this Samaritan woman.

Their conversation started casually with Jesus asking the woman for a drink of water. This request alone should have alerted the woman that something significant was going to happen. It was culturally inappropriate for a man to speak with a woman in public. Drinking out of the woman's cup would have also made Jesus ceremonially unclean.

This wasn't an issue for Jesus, however. He was known for touching the untouchable and giving hope to the hopeless. Before long, Jesus shifted the conversation from physical water that satisfies natural thirst to living water that satisfies spiritual thirst.

Jesus was a master at taking a conversation from the natural to the spiritual. As soon as the Samaritan woman expressed interest in his mention of living water that leads to eternal life, Jesus asked her to go and get her husband. Before delving deeper into spiritual matters, Jesus confronted her lifestyle.

Jesus knew all about the Samaritan woman. Many people in her town would also have known about this woman. With five husbands in her past and a current live-in boyfriend, she would have had an extensive network of ex-family members and friends. Perhaps she was a loose woman; many have speculated as much, but we don't know. If she was, then when she told the people in the village, "Come and see a man who told me everything I ever did!" that could have brought fear to many men in town. In exposing the Samaritan woman, Jesus would be exposing them too.

The response of the townspeople matched the response of the woman. They weren't trying to hide and pretend they were something they were not. Instead, they were willing to be exposed. They humbly acknowledged their need for the Savior.

In contrast, Matthew tells us the account of two demon-possessed men in the region of the Gadarenes. Jesus casts demons out of the men and into a herd of pigs feeding in the distance:

> The whole herd rushed down the steep bank into the sea and drowned in the waters. The herdsmen fled, and going into the city, they told everything, especially what had happened to the demon-possessed men. And behold, all the city came out to meet Jesus, and when they saw him, they begged him to leave their region (Matt. 8:32-34).

What a difference between the response of the Samaritan townspeople and the response of the people in the region of the Gadarenes. The Samaritans begged him to stay while the other townspeople begged him to go away.

The Samaritans heard his message and believed. From the beginning of Jesus' ministry, the message he preached was "Repent, for the kingdom of heaven is at hand" (Matt. 4:17).

When you're confronted with your sin, what's your response? Like the people in the Gadarene region, do you send Jesus away, unwilling to confront the sin in your life and to turn from it? Or are you like the Samaritans who were willing to have their sin exposed so they could follow Jesus in humility?

Jesus still offers living water today to all who repent of their sins and believe.

A Challenge to Religious Beliefs: Nicodemus (John 3:1-21)

Pharisees were known for their strict adherence to the law. They made great efforts to obey the Torah (the five books of Moses, Genesis through Deuteronomy), as well as the oral law.

When we think of the law of Moses, most of us think of the Ten Commandments. In reality, however, those Ten Commandments were just a small fraction of the hundreds of commandments that were given.

Traditionally, Jews believed that when God gave Moses the written law on Mount Sinai, he also verbally gave him other laws to clarify the written laws. These oral laws are referred to in the Gospels as "traditions of the elders" and are now contained in what is known as the Mishnah.

Mosaic law says that one must refrain from work on the Sabbath (Ex. 20:8-11). Oral law, however, breaks that down into thirty-nine prohibited activities, including sowing, plowing, reaping, binding sheaves, threshing, and winnowing.[1]

According to the tradition of the elders, reaping is work. Plucking a handful of grain is reaping, and therefore the Pharisees argued that Jesus' disciples were guilty of breaking the Sabbath (Matt. 12:1-2).

Most of Jesus' interactions with the Pharisees were negative, so it's no wonder that Nicodemus, who was a Pharisee, came to Jesus by night.

Jesus reserved his harshest criticism for the Pharisees. He called them hypocrites, blind guides, blind fools, whitewashed tombs, snakes, and sons of vipers.

The Gospel of John tells us, "Many believed in his name when they saw the signs that he was doing" (John 2:23). It appears that Nicodemus was one of the many who began to trust in Jesus. Just a few verses later, we read these words of Nicodemus to Jesus: "Rabbi, we know that you are a teacher come from God, for no one can do these signs that you do unless God is with him" (John 3:2).

Jesus then tells Nicodemus, "Unless you are born again, you cannot see the Kingdom of God" (John 3:3 NLT).

Like many today, Nicodemus had been trusting in his religious observance. As a Pharisee, he would have had all the outward trappings of religion. He realized, however, that something was missing, and he sought out Jesus to find answers.

Jesus told Nicodemus that he had to be born again. Nicodemus clearly did not understand what he meant.

A new birth would involve a brand-new beginning. For

someone who'd given his life to becoming a high-ranking Jewish leader, this would be difficult to comprehend. To hear that all his past efforts counted for nothing would have been hard to take.

It would have been equally hard for the Israelites in Moses' day to comprehend that they could be saved from death from a serpent's fiery bite only by looking at the bronze serpent Moses had placed on a pole (Num. 21:9).

Jesus was asking Nicodemus to believe by faith that Jesus was the Messiah, and therefore the one who could offer eternal life. For Nicodemus, this would mean recognizing that all his human efforts to keep the law were futile. To be born again would mean starting from scratch. It would mean admitting he was wrong.

In John's account of this encounter, Jesus does most of the talking, and there's no indication of how Nicodemus responded. We do, however, meet Nicodemus two more times in this Gospel.

In John 7, we find Nicodemus standing up for Jesus. The crowds were divided over whether Jesus was indeed the Messiah. Nicodemus boldly states, "Does our law judge a man without first giving him a hearing and learning what he does?" (John 7:51). For this, he's belittled by his peers.

Then in John 19, after the death of Jesus, Nicodemus is with Joseph of Arimathea, preparing the body of Jesus for burial. Nicodemus brings about seventy-five pounds of perfumed ointment made from myrrh and aloes. They wrap the body of Jesus in linen cloths and lay Jesus in the tomb.

It's possible that as Nicodemus watched Jesus die on the cross, he remembered these words Jesus spoke to him: "As Moses lifted up the serpent in the wilderness, so must the Son of Man be lifted up, that whoever believes in him may have eternal life" (John 3:14-15).

It appears from Scripture that Nicodemus was indeed born again. But his keeping of the law and outward show of religion wasn't what made him right with God. The only hope for him is the same as our only hope: "Unless you are born again, you cannot see the Kingdom of God" (John 3:3 NLT).

The Undoing of Father Bart Brewer

While strict adherence to the law was the stumbling block for Nicodemus, loyalty to Rome was the stumbling block for Bart Brewer.[2]

Bart grew up next door to a Dominican convent, and at age sixteen he entered a Catholic seminary in Wisconsin. Twelve years later, he was ordained a Roman Catholic priest in the Discalced Carmelite Order, an order dedicated to a life of prayer and devotion to the Virgin Mary. His greatest desire was to increase the church and to live and die as a Catholic priest.

After about five years, he realized he wasn't at peace with either God or himself. His soul felt dry; he began to feel impatient when listening to confessions, giving penance, and saying mass. He wondered what good he'd done when he blessed such things as plaster figurines, tools, and cars, or sprinkled holy water on baby cribs.

At times he would whip himself or sleep on plywood to mortify his body. He was taught that self-denial and pain would purify his soul.

When a friend pointed out to Bart the contradictions between Christ's teachings and Catholic dogma, Bart had nothing more to do with that friend. When someone challenged the dogma of purgatory as being unscriptural, Bart wouldn't listen. According to the Second Vatican Council, Scripture and dogma were to be treated equally.[3] This meant that to go against a church dogma was not something to be done lightly.

Bart was trying with all his strength to earn his salvation through the church and the sacraments, since he was taught they were necessary for salvation. But the more Bart tried to earn his salvation, the less certain he became. He began to question the scriptural support for the sacraments of penance and the confessional when he couldn't prove them in Scripture.

As he studied the Scriptures, he noticed disagreement between church dogma and the Word of God. He wondered why the church had departed so far from Scripture and why tradition had become more important than simple faith. Faced with his doubts about the authority of the Roman Catholic Church, he realized he needed to leave the church. At the age of thirty-eight, Bart Brewer left the priesthood with just one goal in mind—to do God's will.

The emptiness and restlessness in his soul remained, however, as he realized he was lost. He realized he had only an intellectual knowledge of God, and that his mere mental assent to the message of the gospel was not the same as surrendering his heart and life to Christ. Finally, Bart repented of his sin, renounced his own self-righteousness, accepted the forgiveness that comes through Christ alone, and was born again.

The only hope for Bart and for Nicodemus is also the only hope for us: "Unless you are born again, you cannot see the Kingdom of God" (John 3:3 NLT).

A Challenge to Priorities: The Rich Young Ruler (Matthew 19:16-22)

The Bible gives us an account of a young man described as a rich young ruler. Jesus didn't have to pursue this man; he came running to Jesus. There were no introductions, no small talk. The man just immediately blurted out what was on his heart: "What must I do to have eternal life?"

This would be a dream encounter for anyone who's sharing his or her faith. But had this encounter happened today, a typical Christian might respond to the man by saying, "All you have to do is ask Jesus to come into your heart. Tell him you're sorry for your sin, and ask him to forgive you."

But that's not what Jesus did. Rather Jesus told this man he needed to "keep the commandments."

"Which ones?" the man asked.

And Jesus said, "You shall not murder, You shall not commit adultery, You shall not steal, You shall not bear false witness, Honor your father and mother, and, You shall love your neighbor as yourself."

The young man answered that he'd obeyed all these commandments. "What else must I do?"

Jesus said, "If you would be perfect, go sell what you possess and give to the poor, and you will have treasure in heaven; and come, follow me."

When the young man heard this, he went away sorrowful, for he had great possessions.

How could Jesus let this man get away? He came with urgency—he came *running*. He came with humility—he came kneeling (Mark 10:17).

"And Jesus, looking at him, loved him" (Mark 10:21). But Jesus didn't chase after him.

Why did Jesus tell the young man to sell all his possessions? Is that a requirement for salvation?

No, it is not. We see that in this next encounter.

A Challenge to Priorities: Zacchaeus

In Luke 19, we find the account of Zacchaeus, the chief tax collector, who was very rich. He was so short that he had to climb a tree to see Jesus. Jesus called him down from the tree and said, "I must stay at your house today" (Luke 19:5). Once again, we have a divine appointment. Jesus had to go through Samaria to meet the Samaritan woman, and here Jesus says, "I *must* be a guest in your home today."

Zacchaeus had heard Jesus preach. The passage makes it clear that he had accepted the Lord's message and believed. Zacchaeus proved his belief by his actions. He told the Lord, "The half of my goods I give to the poor" (Luke 19:8).

Jesus responded, "Today salvation has come to this house, since he also is a son of Abraham" (Luke 19:9).

Notice that Zacchaeus didn't give everything away. Jesus asked the rich young ruler to sell all his possessions, but not Zacchaeus. Jesus could see the rich young ruler's heart and knew that his wealth was a higher priority to him than following Jesus. Likewise, Jesus tells all of us, "No servant can serve two masters, for either he will hate the one and love the other, or he will be devoted to the one and despise the other. You cannot serve God and money" (Luke 6:13).

The rich young ruler's response to being told to sell his possessions demonstrated that he wasn't really keeping the law. When Jesus was asked to identify the greatest commandment in the law, he replied, "You shall love the Lord your God with all your heart and with all your soul and with all your mind. This is the great and first commandment. And a second is like it: You shall love your neighbor as yourself. On these two commandments depend all the Law and the Prophets" (Matt. 22:36-40).

Rather than maintain his innocence, the rich young ruler needed to acknowledge that he was incapable of keeping the law. Had he done that, Jesus could have offered him the hope of eternal life apart from the law.

The rich young ruler was trusting in his goodness for salvation. If he'd only said to Jesus, "I haven't fully kept God's law; now what?" then Jesus could have shown him a better way—the only way possible for sinful man!

As long as we try to justify ourselves and our behavior, we can never be justified by God.

"Blessed are the poor in spirit, for theirs is the kingdom of heaven" (Matt. 5:3). The kingdom of heaven is only for those who recognize their spiritual bankruptcy.

The Samaritan woman and her neighbors came to realize that Jesus was the Savior of the world, and they put their trust in him. Jesus exposed her sinful lifestyle; this was her hindrance to salvation. The woman didn't deny her sin; instead, she acknowledged it.

The rich young ruler sadly denied his sin and forfeited eternal life.

In 2016 I went with my husband, Brad, to China with the Gideons. We had the privilege of distributing thousands of Bibles during meetings in several churches. At one of the first churches we visited, our teammate Paul preached to the congregation with our interpreter's help.

After the service, a man with an amulet necklace approached our interpreter and told him, "I've tried everything, and now I want to try Jesus."

Our Chinese interpreter told him, "First, you need to get rid of all your idols." He did not say, "Great! You want Jesus? Repeat this prayer after me, and you'll have Jesus!"

Jesus isn't just an appendage to our lives. Becoming a disciple of Jesus is a serious calling.

While we might think it's okay to hang onto some questionable lifestyle issues, or put our hopes in our religious activities, or give Jesus some place other than first, Jesus makes it clear that we must count the cost to be his disciple. He doesn't want just a part of us; he wants all of us.

REMEMBER

As long as we try to justify ourselves and our behavior, we can never be justified by God.

Ask Yourself

1. What areas of your lifestyle would Jesus be likely to challenge?

2. When confronted about sin in your life, how do you respond? Are you willing to turn from it as the Samaritan woman did, or are you like those from the region of the Gadarenes who sent Jesus away?

3. In following Jesus, are you willing to forsake the things that don't conform to his standards?

4. Are you putting your faith in your religious deeds?

5. The rich young ruler was unwilling to give up his possessions. Is there anything in your life that you're unwilling to give up for Jesus?

CHAPTER THREE

Follow Me

Go therefore and make disciples of all nations.
Matthew 28:19

Great stock is placed in the last words of famous people.

Actor, singer, and teen idol David Cassidy died in 2017. Once the world's highest-paid entertainer, his official fan club was larger than those of Elvis Presley and the Beatles. In a recorded phone conversation, Cassidy spoke of his alcoholism and admitted, "I did it to myself to cover up the sadness and the emptiness." His daughter Kate revealed that his last spoken words were, "So much wasted time."[1]

His early life was enviable by many people's standards, yet his life was ended prematurely by alcoholism. In the end, he wished he'd made better use of his time. There's a lesson there for each of us.

Jesus, on the other hand, truly lived a life of no regrets. Each moment of his life was intentional, and every word spoken was chock-full of significance.

After rising from the dead, Jesus appeared to his disciples. On his last encounter with them before ascending into heaven, He gave them a charge. These are the last words of Jesus:

All authority in heaven and on earth has been given

to me. Go therefore and make disciples of all nations, baptizing them in the name of the Father and of the Son and of the Holy Spirit, teaching them to observe all that I have commanded you. And behold, I am with you always, to the end of the age (Matt. 28:18-20).

There are so many different topics Jesus could have chosen. He could have given instructions to the church or encouraged his disciples to love one another. He chose neither of these, nor countless other directions he could have gone in. Instead, he commanded his disciples to go and make disciples.

The word *disciple* is found well over two hundred times in the New Testament. All these references are in the Gospels and the book of Acts.

What does it mean to be a disciple? Perhaps a better question: What did this mean to those who were called to be disciples in the time of Christ?

The History of Discipleship

The concept of discipleship first came about during the time of the Babylonian captivity when a group was formed known as the Men of the Great Assembly, consisting of 120 members. In time this group would include Ezra, Nehemiah, Daniel, Haggai, Zechariah, and Malachi, as well as Mordecai, the uncle of Queen Esther.

After returning from captivity, the Jews had to rebuild not only the temple and the city walls but also themselves. Corporate worship, prayer, and public reading from the Scriptures all had to be reestablished, as well as their identity as Jews. The Men of the Great Assembly helped them to do that.

The synagogue as well as discipleship—as we see it modeled in the Gospels—were born during this time in history.

The word *synagogue* is a Greek word. In Hebrew, it's called the *Beit Midrash*—the House of Study. It was a place where people could come to hear the Torah read, and teachers would explain its meaning.[2]

The Torah, along with the oral traditions, were studied in the synagogue. The oral traditions were eventually compiled in the second century into what is known today as the Mishnah, as mentioned earlier.

The following passage from the Mishnah gives us some insight into the importance of discipleship.

> Moses received the Torah from Sinai and transmitted it to Joshua; Joshua to the elders; the elders to the prophets; and the prophets handed it down to the Men of the Great Assembly. They said three things: Be deliberate in judgment, raise up many disciples, and make a fence around the Torah.[3]

In another passage from the Mishnah, we're given a glimpse into what Jewish education likely looked like during the time of Christ:

> At five years old [one is fit] for the Scripture, at ten years the Mishnah (oral Torah, interpretations) at thirteen for the fulfilling of the commandments, at fifteen the Talmud (making Rabbinic interpretations), at eighteen the bride-chamber, at twenty pursuing a vocation, at thirty for authority (able to teach others).[4]

This background gives us a clearer understanding of the Gospels.

Like most boys, Jesus was well versed in the Torah, having studied and memorized it. Unlike most boys, however, Jesus had wisdom beyond his years. We see this in his interactions at age twelve with religious teachers in the temple (Luke 2:39-52). To learn from the rabbis, Jewish boys were trained to listen and ask questions. This is what Jesus was doing. "And all who heard him were amazed at his understanding and his answers" (Luke 2:47).

Jesus began his public ministry at age thirty, which is in keeping with the timeline given in the Mishnah. It was then that he began to teach with authority and to call disciples to follow him (Matt. 7:29, Mark 1:21, 22).

The Hebrew word for disciple is *talmid*, and it means "student." The term *rabbi* means "my master." The relationship between a disciple and a rabbi was one of a learner with a teacher, a servant with a master. It could be even closer than a father-son relationship.[5]

A disciple not only loved and honored his rabbi like a father, but he would also seek to imitate every aspect of his rabbi's life. How did he eat his food? How did he walk? How did he address people? How did he pray, and how often? When did he go to bed at night? When did he awake? The goal was to perfectly reflect every aspect of his rabbi's life.

Each disciple came to a rabbinic relationship with a desire and a willingness to surrender to the authority of God's Word as interpreted by his rabbi's view of Scripture.[6] He was in complete surrender to the will and ways of his teacher. "A disciple is not above his teacher, but everyone when he is fully trained will be like his teacher" (Luke 6:40).

The way it typically worked in the time of Christ was that the disciple would choose a rabbi to follow and to pattern his life after (see Mark 5:19; Luke 9:57).

It was the rabbi's job to clarify God's laws as given in the Torah. Some rabbis of that time, like Shammai, interpreted the Scriptures literally, according to the letter of the law; others, such as Hillel, interpreted according to the spirit of the law.[7]

With such different interpretive styles between rabbis, choosing the right rabbi would have been an extremely important decision.

In the Gospels, we see Jesus choosing his disciples, instead of the other way around.

We read that when Jesus called Simon Peter and his brother Andrew, "immediately they left their nets and followed him" (Matt. 4:20). Likewise, when Jesus called James and John, who were in a boat mending nets with their father, "immediately they left the boat and their father and followed him" (Matt. 4:22).

Here we see first-century discipleship in action. These men left everything to follow Jesus. They left both vocation and family.

Jesus said, "If anyone comes to me and does not hate his own father and mother and wife and children and brothers and sisters, yes, and even his own life, he cannot be my disciple" (Luke 14:26). The use of the word *hate* here can cause alarm for those in our culture today. For those in first-century Galilee, however, it was another story. This type of idiom was understood to express the extremeness of the love and commitment demanded by Jesus. Any other affections would appear as hatred in contrast to the extreme love for their Rabbi Jesus.

This is radical discipleship! But were these words intended only for Christ's first-century disciples? Or are they intended for us today as well?

Becoming a disciple of Jesus is a serious matter and not to be entered into lightly. Jesus says that we must count the cost (Luke 14:28-32).

Francis Chan has rightly stated, "Many have come to believe that a person can be a 'Christian' without being like Christ. A 'follower' who doesn't follow. How does that make any sense?"[8]

Today discipleship is often boiled down to a six-week course that's taken after a person's conversion.

In the early church, all disciples were Christians, and all Christians were disciples. "In Antioch the disciples were first called Christians" (Acts 11:26).

Recall again our command from Jesus: "Go and make disciples of all nations...teaching them to obey everything I have commanded you" (Matt. 28:19-20 NIV). In *Making Disciples Jesus' Way,* Doug Greenwold says:

> To the Hebrew mind, "making disciples" was a seamless reality, a continuous process that started with conversion and progressed to teaching followers of Jesus Christ to obey all that he commanded. To the modern Western mind, "making disciples" became something that needed to be broken down into two constituent parts: evangelism (the "saving" of people) and discipleship (the lifelong process of maturing them in Christ). Rather than keeping that Hebrew phrase "make disciples" as a unified thought, Western thought patterns created two new pieces, and then labeled them

"evangelism" and "discipleship"—two new words not found in the Bible! In so doing, it separated that which was intended to be seamless.[9]

Only when we understand what first-century discipleship looked like can each of us answer this question: Am I a disciple of Jesus?

REMEMBER

Our love for Christ must be so extremely great that any other affections would appear as hatred by comparison.

Ask Yourself

1. Do you feel that the "Remember" statement above is too extreme?

2. Based on how you live, who do you love the most in your life? Yourself? Another person? A cause? Or Jesus?

3. If you were brought to trial for being a Christian, would there be enough evidence to convict you?

4. What does being a "disciple" mean to you?

5. What do you think it means to "count the cost" before you become a disciple of Christ?

CHAPTER FOUR

Examine Your Belief

All who believe in him are made right with God
Romans 10:4

J ack couldn't remember a time when he didn't believe
in God. He grew up heavily involved in church life,
beginning in Sunday school. At age nine he prayed to
accept Christ as his Savior after an invitation was given at
vacation Bible school. At age seventeen he was baptized.

He went on to become his church's youth leader, a
position he held for many years. In his thirties he took up
the guitar, and before long he was a regular on the worship
team. It wasn't uncommon for him to take the pulpit when
the lead pastor was on vacation. His sermons were always
well received by the congregation.

At age fifty, Jack died suddenly of a heart attack. He
stood before Jesus and heard these words: "I never knew
you; depart from me."

How could this be? Does such a story sound far-fetched?
Although Jack is a fictional character, he represents one of
the "many" who Jesus tells to depart, because he never
knew them. Although Jack appeared to have a relationship
with Jesus, God saw his heart. Jack had deceived not only
others but also himself.

"These people honor me with their lips, but their hearts are far from me" (Matt. 15:8).

Many

Recall again these words of Jesus:

> On that day many will say to me, "Lord, Lord, did we not prophesy in your name, and cast out demons in your name, and do many mighty works in your name?" And then will I declare to them, "I never knew you; depart from me, you workers of lawlessness" (Matt. 7:21-22).

The word *many* has been defined as "consisting of or amounting to a large but indefinite number."

In those words above of Jesus, who are the "many"? This passage indicates that they're professing Christians who've been active in their service for the Lord. They prophesied in the name of Jesus, which can mean either foretelling things to come or preaching the Word in his name. They cast out demons and performed miracles in the name of Jesus.

We know that these spectacular manifestations can be performed by the devil as well as by God. Therefore, these signs don't prove that the person performing them was a true believer (Job 1:16,19; 2:7; Ex. 7; Acts 13:6-11).

The people in Matthew 7 were surprised when they heard Jesus say, "I never knew you; depart from me." They believed the right things in their heads, but it never transferred down to their hearts. They were self-deceived. The scary thing about deception is that a person who's deceived doesn't know it.

Many who profess faith in Jesus will hear those seven fateful words: "Depart from me, I never knew you."

Earlier in Matthew 7, Jesus speaks of the broad way, saying that there are "many" who enter by it. The Bible warns us: "There is a way that seems right to a man, but its end is the way to death" (Prov. 14:12).

The Faith That Truly Saves

Does belief in God save?

The answer to this question is clear. "You believe that God is one; you do well. Even the demons believe—and shudder" (James 2:19).

Demons believe in God, and they are not saved.

Jesus said, "I am the way, and the truth, and the life. No one comes to the Father except through me" (John 14:6). This verse makes it clear that a general belief in God is not enough; one must also believe in Jesus.

Does belief in Jesus save?

Several times in the Gospels, when demons encounter Jesus, their response is to cry out, "You are the Son of God" (Matt. 8:29, Mark 3:11, Luke 4:41).

We also find the story of a demon-possessed girl who followed Paul and others, saying, "These men are servants of the Most High God, who proclaim to you the way of salvation" (Acts 16:16-18).

We see therefore that demons believe in Jesus and understand the way of salvation, yet they aren't saved.

So what must you and I believe?

True belief means seeing Jesus for who he really is and seeing yourself for who you really are.

Who is Jesus?
- Jesus is fully God (John 1:1, 14, 8:24, 8:58-59, 10:30-33).
- Jesus is fully man, yet without sin (Heb. 2:17, 4:15, 1 Peter 2:22).

Who is man?
- All human beings are sinners who cannot save themselves (Rom. 3:23, 6:8, Eph. 2:8, 9, 1 Tim. 1:15).

Seeing Jesus for who he really is—and ourselves for who we really are—will lead to further crucial questions:

What did Christ's death and resurrection accomplish?
- Christ died as my substitute. He took the penalty for my sin, which is death (Rom. 6:23, 1 Peter 1:18, 1 John 1:16).
- He is my propitiation (Rom 3:24-25, Heb. 2:17, 1 John 2:2).

Propitiation is a big word that a lot of people don't understand. It simply means to appease or satisfy. We deserve the wrath of God, but Jesus "delivers us from the wrath to come" (1 Thes. 1:10).

Christ's death on the cross satisfied God's requirement for salvation.

When a person is saved, they're saved from the penalty for their sins, which is death (Rom. 6:23). They're saved also from the wrath of God (1 Thes. 1:10).

If I don't act on what I believe to be true, can that belief save me?

James answers that question in his epistle when he says, "Faith by itself if it does not have works, is dead" (James 2:17).

Paul speaks of "the obedience of faith" (Rom. 1:5).

True faith is demonstrated by obedience.

In Titus 1:5, Paul speaks of those who "profess to know God, but they deny him by their works. They are detestable, disobedient, unfit for any good work."

Can there be saving faith without a willingness to surrender and obey?

In Matthew 7, Jesus doesn't bring just bad news; he also tells the good news about entry into the kingdom of heaven, which is granted to "the one who does the will of my Father who is in heaven." In contrast, those who are asked to depart are "workers of lawlessness."

The Bible says, "Believe in the Lord Jesus, and you will be saved" (Acts 16:31). Then also, "For God so loved the world, that he gave his one and only Son, that whoever believes in him should not perish but have eternal life" (John 3:16). These verses are absolutely true. "Your word is truth" (John 17:17).

What must also be remembered is that Scripture must interpret Scripture. It's important not to isolate any verse of Scripture but rather to look at all verses on the topic to see what God is really saying. This is one of the rules of hermeneutics (the study of the principles of interpretation).

Belief in Jesus is a critical component in our salvation; we cannot be saved without it. However, belief alone is not enough.

What's missing in the lives of so many who claim belief in Jesus as Savior is repentance. I recently heard an evangelist describe repentance this way: "It's not just saying, 'I'm sorry for my sin'; it's saying, 'I'm *through* with my sin.'"

REMEMBER

Even demons believe. Many people say they believe in Jesus, yet their lives give no evidence that they're born again.

Ask Yourself

1. Do you believe Jesus is the only way to heaven, as he himself says?

2. Why is the identity of Jesus crucial for salvation?

3. Are there non-negotiables that must be believed for salvation? If so, what are they?

4. Is belief in Jesus as Savior enough for salvation? Why or why not?

5. Do you think it's necessary to act on what we know to be true?

6. Is there belief that leads to salvation as well as belief that does not?

CHAPTER FIVE

Repentance—the Missing Note

*Repentance for the forgiveness of sins
should be proclaimed in his name
to all nations, beginning from Jerusalem.*
Luke 24:47

While belief is essential for salvation, the missing piece in so many people's lives is often repentance.

In his book *Except Ye Repent*, Dr. H. A. Ironside writes, "The doctrine of repentance is the missing note in many otherwise orthodox and fundamentally sound circles today."[1] While this was written in 1937, it's even more obvious today.

Ray Comfort shares an excellent analogy in his *Way of the Master* evangelism training videos.

> Imagine your child is deathly sick, and you've been given medicine that will cure her, but you know the medicine is bitter. So in a sincere effort to help her, you water down the medicine to get rid of that bitter taste. And what you've got may be palatable, it may be easier to swallow, but you are in serious danger of causing it to lose its curative properties, and your child may die.
>
> God has given us the medicine that cures death itself, but when we look at how the

Master Physician administered the medicine, we have to admit it seems to have a rather bitter taste. If we look at the Scriptures, we'll see that Jesus openly spoke about judgment, sin, righteousness, and hell, words rarely heard from the lips of popular preachers today.

What they have done is remove from the message that which seems distasteful in an effort to make the message more palatable. They have removed anything that might have a bitter taste, and so they have removed the bitter-tasting yet vital ingredients of sin, righteousness, and judgment to come and replaced them with the sweet-tasting "God has a wonderful plan for your life." And what's happened? The medicine has lost its curative properties. The modern message may be easier to swallow, we may get more decisions, and more people might join our churches, but we are in danger of these people dying in their sins. In other words, despite the fact they've prayed the prayer, if they're not genuinely born of the Holy Spirit, they'll end up in hell.[2]

Repentance is a critical ingredient in the medicine of the gospel. Without it, there is no salvation. The thread of repentance is woven throughout the New Testament from the book of Matthew right through to the book of Revelation (see Matt. 4:17, Rev. 2:5, 15, 21-22; 3:3, 19).

John the Baptist burst on the scene proclaiming, "Repent, for the kingdom of heaven is at hand" (Matt. 3:2).

Jesus declared, "Among those born of women there has arisen no one greater than John the Baptist" (Matt. 11:11).

John's job as the forerunner of Jesus lasted just months before he was imprisoned. Before John was born, God had chosen him and called him to a special purpose: "He will turn many Israelites to the Lord their God.... He will prepare the people for the coming of the Lord.... He will cause those who are rebellious to accept the wisdom of the godly" (Luke 1:16-17 NLT). All these promises and more were given to John's father, Zechariah, before John was even conceived.

As John's popularity grew, he didn't lose sight of why he was here on this earth. He was the forerunner of Jesus the Messiah, with a specific and God-given job to do, and nothing would distract him from it.

John fulfilled his purpose by being obedient to his calling. He challenged people to repent, and he wasn't afraid to bring this message to one and all. He knew the repentance message was for absolutely everyone. He even called for King Herod to repent of his sin. This didn't go over well, and it ultimately cost John his life.

———————

When John was arrested, the ministry of Jesus began, and he echoed the message of John: "Repent, for the kingdom of heaven is at hand" (Matt. 4:17).

Jesus called twelve men to be his disciples, and they accompanied him as he went from village to village teaching people. Jesus had a purpose. He said, "Let us go on to the next towns that I may preach there also, for that is why I came out" (Mark 1:38).

Nothing would deter Jesus from his mission—he came to preach, and his message was "Repent!"

After his disciples traveled with him for many months, it was finally time for them to go out on their own. "So they went out and proclaimed that people should repent" (Mark 6:12).

John the Baptist called for repentance, Jesus called for repentance, and the disciples called for repentance. Clearly, repentance is a critical part of the gospel.

What Does Repentance Really Mean?

What does *repentance* mean? This word's literal meaning is "a change of mind," but repentance is so much more than that. Repentance is a change of mind and heart leading to a change in behavior. As John the Baptist said, "Bear fruit in keeping with repentance" (Matt. 3:8).

Repentance doesn't receive much emphasis today, since it isn't politically correct to tell people they're sinners whose lives need to change. Many people and churches shy away from this doctrine for fear of giving offense. The Bible tells us, however, that the gospel is an offense, and that it's foolishness to the unsaved (1 Cor. 1:18).

Let's look for a moment at what repentance is *not*. It is not sorrow for sin, and it isn't confession.

Judas, who betrayed Jesus, confessed to the chief priests. He was sorry, and he was seized with remorse. Matthew tells us,

> When Judas, who had betrayed him, saw that
> Jesus was condemned, he was seized with

remorse and returned the thirty pieces of silver to the chief priests and the elders. "I have sinned," he said, "for I have betrayed innocent blood" (Matt. 27:3-5 NIV).

That sounds like repentance. Judas felt remorse, acknowledged his sin, and made restitution. Yet the Bible calls him the "son of perdition," and *perdition* means "eternal damnation" or "utter destruction." This account of Judas highlights how things aren't always what they appear to be.

The apostle Paul tells us, "Godly sorrow brings repentance that leads to salvation and leaves no regret, but worldly sorrow brings death" (2 Cor. 7:10 NIV).

American pastor and author A. W. Tozer lived from 1897 to 1963, yet his book *The Root of the Righteous* is as relevant today as when it was written. It includes these words:

> In the Bible, the offer of pardon on the part of God is conditioned upon intention to reform on the part of man. There can be no spiritual regeneration till there has been a moral reformation. That this statement requires defense only proves how far from the truth we have strayed.
>
> In our current popular theology, pardon depends upon faith alone...
>
> We often hear the declaration, "I do not preach reformation, I preach regeneration." Now we recognize this as being the expression of a commendable revolt against the insipid and unscriptural doctrine of salvation by human effort. But the declaration as it stands

contains real error, for it opposes reformation to regeneration. Actually the two are never opposed to each other in sound Bible theology. The not-reformation-but-regeneration doctrine incorrectly presents us with an either-or. This is inaccurate. The fact is that on this subject we are presented not with an either-or, but with a both-and. The converted man is both reformed and regenerated. And unless a sinner is willing to reform his way of living, he will never know the inward experience of regeneration. This is the vital truth which has gotten lost under the leaves in popular evangelical theology.

The idea that God will pardon a rebel who has not given up his rebellion is contrary both to the Scriptures and to common sense.[3]

Repentance is a key element in the gospel message, as we see in the admonition of John the Baptist to the Pharisees and Sadducees: "Bear fruit in keeping with repentance" (Matt. 3:8). That caution still holds today. True biblical repentance will lead to a changed life.

> ## REMEMBER
>
> Without repentance, there is no salvation. Repentance is a change of mind and heart that leads to a change in behavior.

Ask Yourself

1. Does your life show the fruit of repentance?

2. If so, what have you repented of?

3. Reflect on the difference in your life before and after your profession of faith.

4. If you're still doing the same things after your profession of faith as before, you would be wise to examine yourself.

5. Why do you think repentance is not a popular message?

CHAPTER SIX

Strange Fruit

By their fruit you will recognize them.
Matthew 7:16 NIV

The year was 1939. The room was dark except for the spotlight on Billie Holiday's face. Her eyes were closed, and the room was silent as she began, slowly and passionately, to sing the haunting song that would become her signature.

"Strange Fruit" was a protest song against the inhumanity of racism. Abel Meeropol wrote the poem "Bitter Fruit" after viewing a photograph of two black men who'd been lynched and were hanging from a tree. Its title was later changed to "Strange Fruit" because, as Meeropol said, "Bitter is too baldly judgmental. 'Strange,' however, evokes a haunting sense of something out of joint. It puts the listener in the shoes of a curious observer spying the hanging shapes from afar and moving closer toward a sickening realization."[1]

The gruesome images evoked by this song came to my mind as I considered the necessity for spiritual fruit in the life of a true believer. Strange fruit is present when unrighteousness rather than righteousness is evident in the life of a professing Christian.

The imagery of lynching is horrifying; equally offensive

to a holy God is unrighteousness in the life of a professing Christian. It's something out of joint.

In the Sermon on the Mount, Jesus tells us:

> You will recognize them by their fruits. Are grapes gathered from thornbushes, or figs from thistles? So, every healthy tree bears good fruit, but the diseased tree bears bad fruit. A healthy tree cannot bear bad fruit, nor can a diseased tree bear good fruit. Every tree that does not bear good fruit is cut down and thrown into the fire. Thus you will recognize them by their fruits (Matt. 7:16-20).

From the beginning of time, God established the pattern for living things. Plants yield seed after their kind, and trees bear fruit with seeds in them after their kind (Gen. 1:12). Apple trees cannot bear oranges. In the same way, someone who's born again cannot bear the fruit of unrighteousness. It's contrary to nature.

Does this mean that a Christian cannot commit an unrighteous act? Of course not. None of us will be without sin this side of heaven. What it does mean, however, is that unrighteousness will not be the pattern of our lives.

The apostle Paul lists the qualities produced by the Holy Spirit in a person who belongs to Christ:

> The fruit of the Spirit is love, joy, peace, patience, kindness, goodness, faithfulness, gentleness, self-control; against such things there is no law. And those who belong to Christ Jesus have crucified the flesh with its passions and desires. If we live by the Spirit, let us also keep in step with the Spirit (Gal. 5:22-25).

Immediately before those words, Paul also lists acts of the flesh. If these things are present in the life of a professing believer, they would most certainly appear as strange fruit and should have no place in the life of a believer:

> Now the works of the flesh are evident: sexual immorality, impurity, sensuality, idolatry, sorcery, enmity, strife, jealousy, fits of anger, rivalries, dissensions, divisions, envy; drunkenness, orgies, and things like these. I warn you, as I warned you before, that those who do such things will not inherit the kingdom of God (Gal. 5:19-21).

If you're a professing Christian and yet you're engaging unapologetically in any of these behaviors, I would plead with you to examine yourself.

I would have a difficult time telling the difference between a plum tree and a cherry tree if neither of them had fruit. The leaves are similar, and until there's fruit, it's easy to mistake one for the other. In the same way, it isn't always easy to tell if someone who professes faith has truly been born again.

The ultimate evidence for identifying a cherry tree is the cherries. Likewise, the ultimate test for a person's profession of faith is the kind of fruit revealed in that person's life.

When the crowds came to John to be baptized, he said, "You brood of vipers!… Bear fruits in keeping with repentance" (Luke 3:7-8).

Jesus said, "By this my Father is glorified, that you bear much fruit and so prove to be my disciples" (John 15:8).

In Jesus' parable of the sower and the seed, we find four different responses by those who hear the gospel:

> Listen! Behold, a sower went out to sow. And as he sowed, some seed fell along the path, and the birds came and devoured it. Other seed fell on rocky ground, where it did not have much soil, and immediately it sprang up, since it had no depth of soil. And when the sun rose, it was scorched, and since it had no root, it withered away. Other seed fell among thorns, and the thorns grew up and choked it, and it yielded no grain. And other seeds fell into good soil and produced grain, growing up and increasing and yielding thirtyfold and sixtyfold and a hundredfold. And he said, "He who has ears to hear, let him hear" (Mark 4:3-9).

A person's response to the gospel is determined by the condition of their heart, which is represented by the soil in this parable.

Response 1—Seed on the Hardened Path

There are many who hear the gospel but are completely unresponsive. Their hearts are as hard as the soil on a well-used footpath. It's impossible for the seed of the Word to penetrate; it goes in one ear and out the other.

A few years ago, I heard that the brother of someone I knew was dying of cancer. I didn't know the brother, but I felt compelled to visit and share the gospel with him. We had lunch together, and it was a pleasant visit as he shared some of his journey with me, and I shared how the Lord had worked in my life.

I also pointed him to Scripture and showed him verses that explain the good news of the gospel. I explained how Jesus came to save us from the penalty of sin, which is death. Nothing we do could ever earn us favor in the eyes of God. I made it clear that Jesus is the only way to God.

When it was time for me to leave, I encouraged him to seriously consider what I had shared with him and gave him a Bible. As we were saying our goodbyes, he turned to me and said, "I'll take my chances without Jesus." That was the last time I saw him.

Sadly, the seed of the Word fell onto hard ground.

Response 2—Seed on the Rocky Ground

The seed on rocky ground represents the people who gladly receive the message of the gospel. They're quick to respond to an invitation to ask Jesus into their heart or pray a sinner's prayer. Rocky ground has little soil, so roots are unable to get established. When tribulation and persecution arise, these people fall away.

I once observed someone sharing the gospel with a Hindu family. The presentation lasted only a few minutes. In the end, the family was led in a sinner's prayer.

While they were willing to repeat the prayer, I asked myself: Did they truly understand the gospel? Did they realize there's room for only one God in Christianity? Had they counted the cost of following Jesus? Had they come under conviction by the Holy Spirit? Had they repented of their sins? It's easy to get someone to repeat a prayer. Sadly, however, words alone will not save.

When the seed of the Word falls on rocky ground, there's an immediate response, but roots cannot get established; therefore, there's no growth. Where there's no growth, there's no life.

Response 3—Seed in the Weeds

The seed falling among thorns represents people who hear the Word of God, "but the cares of the world and the deceitfulness of riches and the desires for other things enter in and choke the word, and it proves unfruitful" (Mark 4:19).

They love the world, and this is their number one priority in life. Worldly pleasures choke out God's priority, which is for them to "seek first the kingdom of God and his righteousness" (Matt. 6:33).

Paul describes this group in these words: "They profess to know God, but they deny him by their works. They are detestable, disobedient, unfit for any good work" (Titus 1:16).

Countless numbers in our churches today call themselves Christians yet live lives that are virtually indistinguishable from the rest of the world. Sexual immorality and drunkenness are commonplace among many professing Christians.

According to a 2014 report, 61 percent of Christians said they would have sex before marriage.[2] Many profess faith yet habitually live in ways that contradict biblical standards. The Bible tells us, "Those who do such things will not inherit the kingdom of God" (Gal. 5:21). This is a sobering passage. These are not my words, but rather God's Word and his standard. But the good news is there is forgiveness available to all who repent.

Response 4—Seed in Good Ground

The seed that falls on good ground finds soil that's cultivated and ready to receive the seed. The conditions are right for growth, and the seed grows. Not only does it grow, but it produces a crop—thirty, sixty, or even a hundred times what was sown.

Of all the seed that fell, this is the only seed that landed on good soil and developed substantial roots. It's also the only seed that produced fruit.

When the seed of God's Word takes root in our lives, we'll never be the same again.

Charles Spurgeon said, "The same sun which melts wax hardens clay. And the same gospel which melts some persons to repentance hardens others in their sins."[3]

Each of us must ask ourselves: Am I bearing the beautiful fruit of righteousness that's in keeping with someone who professes faith in the Lord Jesus? Or am I bearing strange fruit that's a stench in the nostrils of a holy God?

Jesus said, "My true disciples produce much fruit. This brings great glory to my Father" (John 15:8 NLT).

If this chapter leaves you feeling hopeless—read on.

REMEMBER

A good tree *cannot* bear bad fruit. In the same way, someone who's born again cannot bear the fruit of unrighteousness.

Ask Yourself

1. Reread the list of bad fruit in Galatians 5:19-21. Are any of these things present in your life?

2. Reread Galatians 5:22-25. Which fruit of the Spirit is evidenced in your life?

3. How would you characterize the soil of your heart? Is it hardened, rocky, full of weeds—or fertile ground?

4. How do you think we can make the soil of our hearts more receptive to God's Word?

5. Why do you think many professing believers live in ways that contradict biblical standards, especially in the area of sexual sin?

CHAPTER SEVEN

Confession

*Whoever conceals their sins does not prosper, but the
one who confesses and renounces them finds mercy.*
Proverbs 28:13 NIV

When I share the gospel with someone, I'll often ask,
"Do you think you'll go to heaven when you die?"
Invariably, their answer is yes.

I then ask the follow-up question: "Why should God
let you into heaven?"

Once again, I usually receive the predictable answer:
"Because I'm a good person."

Many people think their goodness will get them into
heaven. The reality, however, is different. The prerequisite
for heaven is found not by proclaiming one's goodness but
rather acknowledging one's badness, accompanied by a
repentant heart.

King David was guilty of some of the same dark sins
that God's Word tells us will bar us from the kingdom
of heaven. He was an adulterer and murderer—yet God
still called him "a man after my own heart." How is that
possible?

A beautiful thing about God is that our sin will not
keep us from a relationship with him, but rather our
attitude toward our sin and how we deal with it.

Although David initially ignored his sin, when

confronted by the prophet Nathan, he confessed it without making excuses or trying to explain it away. He was a man of great passion; this was his strength. But it was also his weakness when his passion was focused in the wrong direction. David knew God. He wasn't deluded into thinking that he was okay when he was not.

The Greek word translated as "confess" in the New Testament means "to say the same thing as another."[1] In other words, when I confess my sin, I agree with God that what he calls sin really is sin. Only when I see God for who he truly is will I see and understand the depths of my sin.

Many today have a skewed idea about sin—that it's no big deal. In reality, sin is a huge deal. Unless a person agrees with God about his sin—confesses his sin—he cannot be saved. Jesus said, "I have come to call not those who think they are righteous, but those who know they are sinners and need to repent" (Luke 5:32 NLT).

David knew he was a sinner. Psalm 51 shows us his heart. It was written after Nathan confronted him about his adultery with Bathsheba. David was broken over his sin and cried out to God for mercy and forgiveness:

> Wash me clean from my guilt.
>> Purify me from my sin.
> For I recognize my rebellion;
>> it haunts me day and night.
> Against you, and you alone, have I sinned;
>> I have done what is evil in your sight.
> You will be proved right in what you say,
>> and your judgment against me is just....
> The sacrifice you desire is a broken spirit.
>> You will not reject a broken and repentant heart,
>> O God (Ps. 51:2-4, 17 NLT).

Chuck Swindoll, in his book *David: A Man of Passion and Destiny,* writes this:

> God is looking for men and women whose hearts are completely His—completely. That means there are no locked closets. Nothing's been swept under the rug. That means when you do wrong, you admit it and immediately come to terms with it. You're grieved over wrong. You're concerned about those things that displease Him. You long to please Him in your actions. You care about the motivations behind your actions.[2]

⟶•⟵

A confession with an explanation is no confession at all.

Years ago, while I was serving as a missionary in Milan, Italy, my team leader Kiernan approached me to discuss a concern. He informed me that I tended to make excuses rather than accept responsibility. My initial reaction was to feel defensive—surely he didn't know what he was talking about.

I don't remember what I said to him, but I do remember that I eventually allowed myself to consider his words, after which I concluded that his assessment was accurate. Almost thirty years later, that conversation has had a tremendous impact on my life. I'm so conscious now of not making excuses that even if I have a legitimate excuse, I try not to use it.

Sometimes when we make excuses, we end up in the gray area of half-truths. For example, let's say you have an appointment and you need to leave the house by six o'clock to get there on time. At 6:10 you finally get your coat on and are heading out the door when the phone rings. You quickly answer, and tell the person on the other end, "I'm just rushing out the door. Can I call you back later this evening?"

When you arrive for your appointment, the first words out of your mouth are "Sorry I'm late, but I was held up by a phone call just as I was leaving the house."

It's true you had a phone call just as you were leaving the house, but is that the real reason you're late? No.

Or perhaps you leave the house late only to run into heavy traffic that makes you even later. Upon arriving at your destination, do you blame the traffic for being late, or do you own up to the fact that you didn't leave the house on time?

A half-truth is a whole lie.

As Christians, we should be people of integrity in every area of our lives. I've got a long way to go to become the person God wants me to be.

In the situation with my teammate, my first step was to agree that what he said was true.

As important as confession is, however, it's only half of the equation. Let me explain. If a murderer were to stand before a judge and confess to killing his neighbor, that would hardly be satisfactory. A confession is a great first step, but unless it's accompanied by repentance, it falls short.

David confessed his sin and repented of his sin. Psalm 32 expresses his joy of restoration:

Oh, what joy for those
>> whose disobedience is forgiven,
>> whose sin is put out of sight!
Yes, what joy for those
>> whose record the Lord has cleared of guilt,
>> whose lives are lived in complete honesty!
When I refused to confess my sin,
>> my body wasted away,
>> and I groaned all day long.
Day and night your hand of discipline was heavy
on me.
>> My strength evaporated like water in the summer
>> heat.
Finally, I confessed all my sins to you
and stopped trying to hide my guilt.
>> I said to myself, "I will confess my rebellion to the
>> Lord."
And you forgave me! All my guilt is gone (Ps. 32:1-5 NLT).

The reality is that we're all sinners. Some people's sins are more visible than others, but in the eyes of God, sin is sin.

From time to time we hear news reports of people who've been exposed for wrongdoing. More often than not, the person being confronted will deny the allegations.

Such was the case with cyclist Lance Armstrong, seven-time Tour de France winner, who vehemently and continually denied allegations of doping for over ten years. In a videotaped testimony given under oath in 2005, he said, "How many times do I have to say it?... Well, it can't be any clearer than *I've never taken drugs.*"

In 2013, Armstrong finally came clean—in an interview with Oprah Winfrey. He told her he was driven to cheat by a "ruthless desire to win."[3] Later, in a telephone interview with CNN, the disgraced cyclist said, "Once you say no you have to keep saying no. If this stuff hadn't taken place with the federal investigation, I'd probably still be saying no with the same conviction and tone as before. But that gig is up." Despite his admission of guilt, Armstrong said if he went back in time to the beginning of his career, he would "probably do it again."[4]

This is an example of confession without repentance.

In March 2019, stories of a college admissions bribery scandal flooded the news. Of the fifty people indicted in this case, just thirteen pleaded guilty. One of these was actress Felicity Huffman, who made this statement:

> I am pleading guilty to the charge brought against me by the United States Attorney's office. I am in full acceptance of my guilt, and with deep regret and shame over what I have done, I accept full responsibility for my actions and will accept the consequences that stem from those actions…. My desire to help my daughter is no excuse to break the law or engage in dishonesty.[5]

Huffman was willing to admit her guilt for her wrongdoing, and to accept the consequences for her actions. That's refreshing.

It's always sad to hear of a Christian leader who fails morally. It's encouraging, however, when such a leader confesses his fault and repents of his sin.

Such was the case in 1987 when Gordon MacDonald, president of Inter-Varsity Christian Fellowship, resigned after admitting that he'd been in an adulterous relationship. "I need your forgiveness," he said, but he didn't stop there. MacDonald took "the biblically defined steps that call for confession, repentance, and restoration."[6] He submitted to church discipline by the elders of his church, and he was ultimately restored and has gone on in his service for the Lord.

What sets apart a true follower of Jesus from one who follows in word only is a proper response to sin.

When recalling your indiscretions of the past, do you think of them with a twinkle in your eye? Or do you feel sorrow? Do you love your sin, or hate it? Do you cherish it, or do you despise it?

Your relationship with sin is one of the greatest indicators of the reality of your profession.

"If we say we have no sin, we deceive ourselves, and the truth is not in us" (1 John 1:8). For years I read this verse and thought, *No one claims to be without sin; we all know that we mess up sometimes.* Then it finally dawned on me that claiming to be without sin could be taken to refer to specific sins.

While most will admit to being sinners, some will deny that certain things in their lives are sin. "If we say we have not sinned, we make him a liar, and his word is not in us" (1 John 1:10).

Although David initially tried to cover up his adultery with Bathsheba by having her husband killed, when he was confronted about his sin by Nathan the prophet, his immediate response was to confess it, acknowledging that it was God who he'd sinned against. He could have rationalized it, excused it, or redefined it, as many often do. Rather, he was broken over his sin.

"If we confess our sins, he is faithful and just to forgive us our sins and to cleanse us from all unrighteousness" (1 John 1:9).

You can't confess your sin and deny your sin at the same time. God hates sin. Therefore, if I'm to agree with God, I too must hate sin. Anything less is not a true confession, and without confession of sin, there's no forgiveness of sin.

Remember

When we confess our sin, we agree with God that what he calls sin really is sin. It's not our sin that keeps us from a relationship with God—but rather our attitude toward our sin, and how we deal with it.

Ask Yourself

1. What things in your life that God calls sin are you making excuses for?

2. What's the difference between confession and repentance?

3. What is your response when confronted with sin?

4. Are you willing to confess and repent of your sin? What would repentance look like in your life?

5. Why is sin a heart issue, not merely an outward issue?

CHAPTER EIGHT

Forgiveness

*In him we have redemption through his blood, the forgiveness
of our trespasses, according to the riches of his grace.*
Ephesians 1:7

How can the Lord ever forgive me? Helen asked herself
this question. Raised in a Christian home, she'd led
a double life for years. While Helen made a profession of
faith and sang in the choir, her life outside the church walls
was another story.

She became pregnant by her boyfriend, and they felt
they had to get married. After the wedding, she gave birth
to a baby girl. When she found out she was pregnant with
their second child, Helen took an abortion pill to terminate
the pregnancy. Afterward, it was hard for her to imagine
that God could ever forgive her.

Helen later began attending a different church where
she was struck by the love of Christ reflected in the people,
especially in their unconditional love for her.

God finally got hold of her life one Easter weekend,
when she was thirty years old. She kept thinking about
Jesus dying on the cross for her. She felt as if he was still
hanging there, and the cross was blocking her way. She
realized she couldn't go another step with her life until she
decided if she was for him or against him. Finally, she fell

on her knees and said, "Lord, I don't know why you could want me, but if you do, you can have me."

Helen explains in her own words what happened:

> On that Good Friday, I was crucified with Christ, and on that Easter morning, I arose with him. I was filled with the most incredible joy as I sang the Easter songs in church and took the communion rightfully for the first time. I was a new creature, and I knew it![1]

Forgiveness is at the heart of the gospel. Jesus paid for our forgiveness with his own blood. "Without the shedding of blood there is no forgiveness of sins" (Heb. 9:22).

Oswald Chambers wrote,

> The only ground on which God can forgive our sin and reinstate us to His favor is through the Cross of Christ. There is no other way! Forgiveness, which is so easy for us to accept, cost the agony at Calvary.[2]

After we've experienced God's forgiveness, we're in a position to extend forgiveness to one another.

One of my favorite stories of forgiveness is told by Corrie ten Boom in *The Hiding Place*. Corrie and her Dutch family were active in sheltering Jews and resistance workers during World War II. These secret activities were discovered by the Nazis, and they were all arrested.

Corrie and her sister, Betsie, suffered abuse and indignity in concentration camps, including Ravensbruck. While there, Betsie died, but due to a clerical error, Corrie was released in December 1944. A week later, all the women around her age in the camp were sent to the gas chamber.

Following the war, Corrie ten Boom started a

rehabilitation center in the Netherlands. She also traveled extensively, sharing a message of forgiveness. One of her most well-known sayings on forgiveness is this: "When we confess our sins, God casts them into the deepest ocean, gone forever."

Less than three years after her release, she'd just finished her message in a church in Munich, Germany. People had begun filing out when Corrie saw a balding heavyset man in a gray overcoat making his way toward her. He clutched a brown hat in his hands. Suddenly, in her mind, his overcoat and brown hat turned into a blue uniform and visor cap with a skull and crossbones. She recalled being back in Ravensbruck in a large room with harsh overhead lights, where she'd been forced to walk naked past this man, whom she now recognized as a guard at Ravensbruck.

Standing before her in the Munich church, the man extended his hand toward Corrie and said, "A fine message, *fräulein*! How good it is to know that, as you say, all our sins are at the bottom of the sea!"

He didn't seem to remember her, but she remembered him clearly as one of her captors. Her blood seemed to freeze as her hands fumbled in her purse. How glibly she'd spoken of forgiveness moments before.

"You mentioned Ravensbruck in your talk," the man said. "I was a guard there." He went on to tell her how he'd become a Christian, and how he knew God had forgiven him for the cruel things he'd done there. But he wanted to hear it from her as well. For this man, Corrie represented all the people he'd mistreated.

With his hand still reaching out, he asked her, "Will you forgive me?"

Corrie stood there thinking of how God had forgiven her again and again for her own sins, and yet in this moment she couldn't forgive. Simply by asking forgiveness, could this man standing in front of her erase the slow terrible death her sister Betsie had suffered, or all the awful indignities she herself had endured?

She felt as though she stood there for hours instead of seconds as she wrestled with the most difficult thing she ever had to do. Corrie knew she had to forgive. She remembered the words of Jesus: "If you do not forgive, neither will your Father in heaven forgive your trespasses" (Mark 11:26 NKJV).

From her work with those who'd been in the concentration camps, Corrie knew that those who were able to forgive their former enemies were able to resume normal lives in the outside world, while those who couldn't forgive remained like invalids.

Corrie also knew that forgiveness is an act of the will. She prayed silently, "Jesus, help me!" She placed her hand into that of her former captor. In that moment, as she recalls, "healing warmth seemed to flood my whole being, bringing tears to my eyes. 'I forgive you, brother!' I cried. 'With all my heart!'"

They stood there, the former guard and the former prisoner, clasping hands. Corrie ten Boom said, "I had never known God's love so intensely, as I did then."[3]

<hr/>

The ability to forgive is supernatural. When we extend forgiveness, we're being like Jesus. As Paul tells us, "Be kind to one another, tenderhearted, forgiving one another, as God in Christ forgave you" (Eph. 4:32).

Jesus once clarified his teaching on forgiveness after Peter had asked him, "Lord, how often shall I forgive someone who sins against me? Seven times?" Jesus answered him, "No, not seven times, but seventy times seven!" (Matt. 18:21-22 NLT).

Jesus went on to make his point even clearer by telling a parable:

> Therefore, the Kingdom of Heaven can be compared to a king who decided to bring his accounts up to date with servants who had borrowed money from him. In the process, one of his debtors was brought in who owed him millions of dollars. He couldn't pay, so his master ordered that he be sold—along with his wife, his children, and everything he owned—to pay the debt.
>
> But the man fell down before his master and begged him, "Please, be patient with me, and I will pay it all." Then his master was filled with pity for him, and he released him and forgave his debt.
>
> But when the man left the king, he went to a fellow servant who owed him a few thousand dollars. He grabbed him by the throat and demanded instant payment.
>
> His fellow servant fell down before him and begged for a little more time. "Be patient with me, and I will pay it," he pleaded. But his creditor wouldn't wait. He had the man arrested and put in prison until the debt could be paid in full.

> When some of the other servants saw this, they were very upset. They went to the king and told him everything that had happened. Then the king called in the man he had forgiven and said, "You evil servant! I forgave you that tremendous debt because you pleaded with me. Shouldn't you have mercy on your fellow servant, just as I had mercy on you?" Then the angry king sent the man to prison to be tortured until he had paid his entire debt.
>
> That's what my heavenly Father will do to you if you refuse to forgive your brothers and sisters from your heart (Matt. 18:23-35 NLT).

The king's servant did the very thing he'd begged his master not to do to him. After pleading for patience and being granted it, along with mercy, this servant granted nothing when his fellow servant begged for patience.

We, like the king's servant, have an immeasurable debt. Our debt of sin is beyond our ability to pay. We need our merciful King Jesus to step in and forgive our debt. Often we demand justice for others but want mercy for ourselves.

It's important to understand not only what forgiveness is, but also what it is not. Forgiveness doesn't mean condoning or excusing an offense. Forgiveness doesn't say that the wrong committed was okay.

Forgiveness isn't always easy, especially when the hurt runs deep. However, any offense I've suffered pales in comparison to my offense against a holy God.

A recent example of forgiveness occurred at the time I was writing this chapter. It happened on October 2, 2019, during the trial of former Dallas police officer Amber Guyger. After entering what she mistakenly thought was her own apartment, she shot and killed Botham Jean, thinking he was an intruder. Brandt Jean, younger brother of the victim, had the courtroom in tears when he took the stand for his victim impact statement. He said,

> I hope you go to God with all the guilt, all the bad things you may have done in the past. Each and every one of us may have done something we're not supposed to do. If you're truly sorry, I know, I can speak for myself, I forgive you. And I know, if you go to God and ask him, he will forgive you…. I love you just like anyone else…. I personally want the best for you…. The best would be—give your life to Christ.[4]

Whoopi Goldberg of ABC's *The View* reacted to the story the following day by saying,

> Sometimes it hits you to think, *Now that's Christian,* because how many people call themselves that and will allow things to go on? But here's this kid who says, "I don't want you to rot in hell, I want your life to be good…. I forgive you."[5]

Each of us is responsible to God only for ourselves, and we're commanded to forgive others. As John Piper says,

> Struggling to forgive is not what destroys us. As long as we are in the flesh, we will do our good deeds imperfectly, including forgiving and loving others. Jesus died to cover those imperfections. What destroys us is the settled position that we are not going to forgive, and we have no intention to forgive, and we intend to cherish the grudge and fondle the wrong that someone did to me and feel the bitterness.

> It feels good. I like to go to bed with my wrath
> at night because he legitimately wronged me. I
> am going to hold this against him for the rest
> of his life. If we think we can be indwelt by
> the Spirit of Christ and not make war on that
> attitude, we are deluded.[6]

Before we're able to forgive others, we need to truly grasp the depravity of our own hearts and the mountain of sin that we need to deal with personally. Once we've dealt with our own sin against a holy God, we're in a position to extend forgiveness to others.

Forgiveness is a part of the character of God; if we're his disciples, it will be a part of our character also.

REMEMBER

Forgiveness is at the heart of the gospel, because Jesus paid for our forgiveness with his own blood. The ability to forgive is supernatural; when we extend forgiveness, we're being like Jesus.

Ask Yourself

1. Is there something in your life that you feel God can't forgive you for?

2. Being forgiven ourselves frees us to forgive others. Is there someone you need to forgive?

3. Think of something that God has forgiven you for.

4. Why do you think God *commands* us to forgive, rather than making it optional?

5. Does forgiveness condone or excuse an offense? Why or why not?

CHAPTER NINE

Examine Your Obedience

And we can be sure that we know him
if we obey his commandments.
1 John 2:3 NLT

One of the tests of true faith is obedience. We can be sure we know the Lord if we obey his commandments. The flip side of this is that if we don't obey his commandments, we cannot be sure we know him.

John 3:16 is a verse frequently quoted to show our need to believe to be saved. This verse in the *New Living Translation* reads: "For this is how God loved the world: He gave his one and only Son, so that everyone who believes in him will not perish but have eternal life." Then later in the same chapter we find this verse: "Anyone who believes in God's Son has eternal life. Anyone who doesn't obey the Son will never experience eternal life but remains under God's angry judgment" (John 3:36 NLT).

There's a definite connection here between belief and obedience. This is not an isolated passage; in fact, we find this connection throughout both the Old and New Testaments.

I'm not saying our good works save us. The Bible is quite clear on that subject. "God saved you by his grace when you believed. And you can't take credit for this; it is a gift from God. Salvation is not a reward for the good things we have done, so none of us can boast about it" (Eph. 2:8-9 NLT). We are not saved *by good works* but *for good works,* a truth which is expressed in this verse: "For we are his workmanship, created in Christ Jesus for good works, which God prepared beforehand, that we should walk in them" (Eph. 2:10).

The Bible is clear in its teaching that obedience is the natural outworking of faith. They're two sides of the same coin, and they cannot be separated.

———⸻———

The life of someone whom I'll call Natalie is living proof of the connection between faith and obedience. When she met Jesus, her hunger for God's Word began to grow. As it grew, her desire to be obedient to what she was learning also grew.

The peace, hope, and joy that she was experiencing would make it hard for anyone to imagine that just months before, Natalie was contemplating suicide. Her world was falling apart, and she felt that everyone would be better off without her.

One evening she found herself at a meeting, completely unaware that the message she was going to hear would change her life forever. The speaker was reading from Psalm 139. Natalie was riveted by the words of hope she heard. Did God truly know and understand her completely? Did he love her and have a purpose for her life? Did she dare take the chance to trust him?

Before this moment, Natalie considered herself to be a Christian, having grown up in a liberal Christian environment. She attended church regularly, sang in the choir, volunteered, and knew lots of Bible stories. She also believed that there were many ways to God, and she embraced new age thinking as well as aboriginal spirituality. Evangelical belief was scorned and ridiculed by most folks in her circle.

Natalie responded to the altar call that was given that evening and totally surrendered herself to God. Through Psalm 139, God revealed to Natalie his grace and his love, his understanding, and a promise of hope.

She clearly recalls offering the mess of her life in a desperate prayer: "Oh God, I can't do this."

Immediately, Natalie was filled with a hunger and desire to know the truth. She began spending hours upon hours reading the Bible. Two things were happening simultaneously: While she was growing more hopeful, she was also beginning to grieve. She began to see her sinfulness in a new light. She saw that things she had done were actually sin, not just bad choices or wrong decisions. Often she was flooded by tears, wondering how she could ever be forgiven, yet knowing that she was. She was so grateful, and she desired to be more and more obedient to what God desired.

God's promise that she was now a "new creature" had a profound effect on her. Day after day, week after week, Natalie kept reading and learning. Scripture increasingly became her life's authority as she got to know the Bible and encountered there the revealed will of God. She was driven to do what God wanted. If Scripture said it, she was determined to apply it. At times she simply followed the instructions and moved forward into life-change, but at other times she was overcome with sorrow as she bumped up against her sin.

When she got to the book of Ephesians and discovered

that there was to be no foul language or "worthless talk," it became clear to her that she had to clean up the way she spoke. Not using foul language seemed straightforward, but the broader change of moving away from old habits of worthless talk—including dirty jokes, flirting, and ugly gossip—took a lot longer, and she finds it challenging at times even today.

When she encountered Philippians and the charge to think on the things that are lovely and true and of good report, she realized how important her thought life was. She saw her need to guard what she looked at (movies, books, magazines), what she listened to (music, the talk of others), and especially what she thought about (reasons for bitterness and unforgiveness).

She began to eliminate CDs and videos from her collection that she felt did not meet God's standards as laid out in the Bible. She threw out books and magazines. That process of careful examination continues in her life today.

The words of 1 Peter 3 about the unfailing beauty of a gentle and quiet spirit being precious to God forged a deep longing in Natalie for the fruit of the Spirit to be evident in her. She longed for anger and bitterness to be gone, and she truly endeavored to abide in Jesus and allow his Word to abide in her.

Out of obedience to the Word of God, Natalie began dressing more modestly and presented herself in a gentler way.

There were times when obedience seemed straightforward, but other times were more difficult, especially concerning sins of her heart which were hidden from others but not to God.

Lying was a huge issue for Natalie. She felt incapable

of consistently telling the truth—which meant that she couldn't be trusted, and she trusted no one. She tried to always tell the truth, but failed again and again. She would exaggerate, tell a half-truth, or spin an impression, often without even realizing it until the Lord gently reminded her of a Scripture verse; then she would grieve again. When she failed, she would ask for forgiveness.

Natalie struggled to forgive certain people, but she knew she had to do it. She understood that her sins had been nailed to the cross, and that the Lord remembered them no more. How could she continue rehearsing the wrongs of others? She began personalizing Scripture and spoke it aloud to herself, especially from the love passage in 1 Corinthians 13: "I am patient, I am kind, I keep no record of wrongs, I rejoice in truth…"

Learning to walk in obedience took time for Natalie—as it does for all of us. It's a lifelong pursuit. Her obedience is motivated by the love and thankfulness she has for such incredible mercy and grace.

Natalie has been a follower of Jesus for twenty-one years now, and she continues to find the Lord faithful to his promises. He has exchanged her bitterness and anger for joy, her unforgiveness for a forgiving heart, and her confusion for clarity. He traded her arrogance for a desire for humility. Her rebelliousness has been transformed into a longing to surrender and be obedient to God's plans and purposes. For her foul language, he gave a new language of tears, which she says she now speaks rather fluently. For her hard, selfish heart, God gave a tender one full of gratitude. He has provided godly teachers along the way, and given her a faith family she loves deeply. He has given

Natalie the opportunity to serve within the church, which she finds astonishing.

He hasn't made her life perfect, nor has he removed struggles and difficulties, hardship and stress. But he has comforted and assured Natalie, enabling her to bear the sadness of the natural consequences of past sinfulness. Despite tension, disappointments, and sometimes sufferings, her life now is rich with hope, deep joy, and truth.

The pathway to freedom and hope for Natalie was the path of obedience. She says, "He has not yet finished his work in me. Regrettably, I still offend him and his other children at times, but when I go to him and ask, he's quick to forgive and restore me. His presence is real! His Scriptures are full of life! He daily offers mercy, hope, strength, grace, and peace. To God be the glory!"

We see this connection between faith and obedience in a passage from the book of Hebrews about the Israelites, who did not obey God after Moses led them out of Egypt into the desert:

> And to whom was God speaking when he took an oath that they would never enter his rest? Wasn't it the people who *disobeyed* him? So we see that because of their *unbelief,* they were not able to enter his rest (Heb. 3:18-19 NLT).

What kept them from entering God's rest? Was it their disobedience or their unbelief? It was both—because true faith is evidenced by obedience.

The epistle of James also makes this point clear:

> What good is it, dear brothers and sisters, if you say you have faith but don't show it by your actions? Can that kind of faith save anyone?... How foolish! Can't you see that faith without good deeds is useless? (James 2:14,20 NLT).

John Piper says,

> Works are not the cause of salvation; works are the evidence of salvation. Faith in Christ always results in good works. The person who claims to be a Christian but lives in willful disobedience to Christ has a false or dead faith and is not saved.[1]

Paul begins his letter to the Romans by explaining that his job is to share the good news of the gospel with the Gentiles "so that they will believe and obey him, bringing glory to his name" (Rom. 1:5 NLT).

Our obedience is the fruit of our faith. The faith that justifies is the kind of faith that changes us through the work of the Holy Spirit (Rom. 8:13).

John Piper also says this:

> If your faith in Christ leaves you unchanged, you don't have saving faith. Obedience—not *perfection*, but a new *direction* of thought and affections and behavior—is the fruit that shows that the faith is alive. Faith alone justifies, but the faith that justifies is never alone. It is always accompanied by 'newness of life' (Rom. 6:4).[2]

———

Jesus tells a parable about two sons who are asked by their father to go work in the vineyard (Matt. 21:28-32). The first tells his father that he won't go, but in the end, he spends the day working in the vineyard. The other son says he'll go, but then he doesn't. Jesus then asks, "Which of the two did the will of his father?"

Although the first son initially said he wouldn't work for his father, he later changed his mind and did his father's will. The second son gave lip service to his father, but that's where it ended. This parable teaches us that doing is more important than mere saying.

Scripture shows us that Abraham obeyed God by faith, and his faith was manifested by obedience: "By faith Abraham obeyed when he was called to go out to a place that he was to receive as an inheritance. And he went out, not knowing where he was going" (Heb. 11:8).

Noah showed the same obedience that comes by faith: "It was by faith that Noah built a large boat to save his family from the flood. He obeyed God, who warned him about things that had never happened before. By his faith, Noah condemned the rest of the world, and he received the righteousness that comes by faith" (Heb. 11:7 NLT).

You and I will also obey if our faith is real.

REMEMBER

If we don't obey God's commandments, we can't be sure we know him.

Ask Yourself

1. Are there areas of your life where you know you're being disobedient to God?

2. Can we be saved by doing good deeds?

3. Why is doing more important than just saying?

4. If our faith leaves us unchanged, what does that say about our faith?

5. How did Abraham and Noah manifest their faith?

CHAPTER TEN

Examine Your Loves

Do not love the world or the things in the world.
If anyone loves the world, the love of the Father
is not in him.
1 John 2:15

D o not love the world. What exactly does that mean? The apostle John helps us answer that question in his epistle when he gives us a good description of the world system: "For all that is in the world—the desires of the flesh and the desires of the eyes and pride of life—is not from the Father but is from the world (1 John 2:16).

Satan is the ruler of this world (see John 12:31; 14:30; 16:11), and we're warned against getting entangled with his system:

> Do not conform to the pattern of this world, but be transformed by the renewing of your mind. Then you will be able to test and approve what God's will is—his good, pleasing and perfect will (Rom. 12:2 NIV).

The world is screaming in our ears, telling us how to think, what to do, how to dress, what we should listen to, and what we should watch. Many who claim faith in Christ are blindly following along, believing the lies of Satan, the father of lies (John 8:44).

The World's Entertainment

As believers, our standard for what constitutes good entertainment should be different from the world's standard.

Does it seem right that those who profess faith in Christ entertain themselves with things that God hates? You would be hard-pressed to find a movie today that doesn't feature characters engaging in sexual immorality, either premarital or extramarital. This is so commonplace that many professing Christians don't even blink an eye.

John Wesley, who lived in the eighteenth century, said, "What one generation tolerates, the next generation will embrace."[1] Is this not true? Some things accepted within the church today would have been scandalous even outside of the church fifty years ago.

Consider this verse: "It is shameful even to mention what the disobedient do in secret" (Eph. 5:12 NIV). With that standard, you might think we could never go to the movies or watch TV. But the question each of us needs to be asking ourselves is not "Could I?" but "Should I?"

Paul tells us that many things are allowed, but not all things are beneficial or constructive (1 Cor. 10:23). He also says, "Whatever you do, do all to the glory of God" (1 Cor. 10:31). Concerning the things we watch, we should be taking time to ask ourselves, "Does this show bring glory to God? What would Jesus do? What would Jesus watch?"

If you can watch a show with a clear conscience toward God, that's great. If not, then a good rule of thumb is: When in doubt, don't.

Reading that, some people might accuse me of legalism. But I'm not telling anyone what to do or how to live. I'm merely pointing out Scripture that encourages holy living, to which all true followers of Christ are called.

There aren't two classes of Christians, those who strive to lead holy lives and those who said a prayer yet continue to live a worldly lifestyle. No, we're all exhorted to "strive... for the holiness without which no one will see the Lord" (Heb. 12:14).

Years ago, I asked a man, "Are you a Christian?"

"Sure I am—just not like you."

What he was really saying was this: "I'm a Christian, but not an extreme one like you." His lifestyle was indistinguishable from the world's.

A transformed life is a mark of a true believer. If your life looks the same after you professed faith as it did before, then you have reason to doubt if your faith is real. "If anyone is in Christ, he is a new creation. The old has passed away; behold, the new has come" (2 Cor. 5:17).

We're exhorted in God's Word to think about things that are "true, honorable, just, pure, lovely, commendable, excellent and worthy of praise" (Phil. 4:8). If the movie or TV show you've chosen to watch encourages these attributes, it's safe to say you can watch with a clear conscience. But if there's content that is impure and not praiseworthy, you do well to find something better to do with your time.

Some who are true believers may frequently entertain themselves with things that offend a holy God. If so, they've bought into the devil's lies and have told themselves, *It's not that bad.*

They aren't letting Scripture guide their entertainment choices, having failed to remember that God's Word is "useful to teach us what is true and to make us realize what is wrong in our lives. It corrects us when we are wrong and teaches us to do what is right. God uses it to prepare and equip his people to do every good work" (2 Tim. 3:16 NLT).

The World's Money

How important is money to you? You might say it's very important, since we all need it to live. But is having money and making money the driving force in your life?

Jesus said, "No one can serve two masters, for either he will hate the one and love the other, or he will be devoted to the one and despise the other. You cannot serve God and money" (Matt. 6:24).

Some years ago, I heard a story of a man on an airplane who ordered a drink. The flight attendant had to leave suddenly before she was able to collect his money. He had two dollars sitting on his tray, waiting for her to return. After a while, he realized she hadn't remembered to collect the money. She passed a few times without looking his way, and eventually he put the money back into his pocket. That man had sold his integrity for two dollars.

One definition of integrity is doing the right thing even when no one's looking. Trading two dollars for a clear conscience doesn't seem like a fair trade, does it?

We should all ask ourselves: "Am I serving God or money?"

Have you ever been asked to pay in cash? Or perhaps you've been the one doing the asking. Often the reason someone asks to be paid in cash is to avoid paying taxes. How about downloading music or movies that we haven't paid for? Or lying about the age of our child to avoid paying the adult price?

What's the motivating factor in our decisions? Saving a few dollars, or honoring God?

What about paying taxes? One day some Pharisees and supporters of Herod came to Jesus with the intent of tricking him, and they asked, "Is it right to pay taxes to Caesar or not?" Jesus said, "Give to Caesar what belongs to Caesar, and give to God what belongs to God" (Mark 12:14, 17 NLT).

Giving to Caesar in those days would be the equivalent of paying taxes to the government in our day. In the book of Romans, Paul tells us the attitude we're to have toward the government:

> Let every person be subject to the governing authorities. For there is no authority except from God, and those that exist have been instituted by God. Pay to all what is owed to them: taxes to whom taxes are owed, revenue to whom revenue is owed, respect to whom respect is owed, honor to whom honor is owed (Rom. 13:1, 7).

It's interesting to note that Nero was the reigning Caesar in power when Paul wrote these words. Nero was known for his cruelty and depravity, yet Paul, through the inspiration of the Holy Spirit, exhorts Christians to treat those in power with respect and honor. It was during the reign of Nero that the apostle Paul was beheaded, according to Christian tradition.

As believers, we shouldn't evade taxes, nor should we aid someone else in doing so. This may cost us financially at times, but how much is a clear conscience worth?

Sadly, there have been times in my life when I've put money before God. Many of us in these situations try to justify our actions. If we're true believers, however, the Holy Spirit will come alongside and bring conviction. We then have a choice: Will we listen to the voice of God or get caught up in the devil's lies?

We need to ask ourselves the hard questions. What's more important: honoring Almighty God, or having more of the almighty dollar?

Remember what Jesus taught us:

> Do not lay up for yourselves treasures on earth, where moth and rust destroy and where thieves break in and steal, but lay up for yourselves treasures in heaven, where neither moth nor rust destroys and where thieves do not break in and steal. For where your treasure is, there your heart will be also (Matt. 6:19-21).

The World's Music

"Guard your heart above all else," we're told in Scripture, "for it determines the course of your life" (Prov. 4:23 NLT). And music is an especially powerful influence on the heart.

In his younger years, my husband, Brad, used to jokingly say, "I know the words to every song ever written." He listened to a lot of music, especially from his favorite band at the time, the Rolling Stones. The lyrics of their songs would constantly be playing in his head.

As he grew in his relationship with the Lord, he finally reached the point where he asked himself, *Do I want Mick Jagger's words running through my mind, or do I want God's words?*

Secular doesn't necessarily equal bad. We must, however, guard our hearts.

A verse from a Sunday school song comes to mind.

Oh, be careful little ears what you hear.
Oh, be careful little ears what you hear.
For the Father up above is looking down in love,
so be careful little ears what you hear.

Music has an upside and a downside. Dietrich Bonhoeffer, the German pastor and theologian, captured the upside when he said, "Music…will help dissolve your perplexities and purify your character and sensibilities, and in time of care and sorrow, will keep a fountain of joy alive in you."[2] Martin Luther said, "Next to the Word of God, music deserves the highest praise."[3] The Psalms are full of lyrics giving praise to God that were written to be sung.

The downside of music is captured in this quote from Tom Waitts: "I like beautiful melodies telling me terrible things."[4]

A survey performed among more than two hundred adolescents revealed there was an association between watching music videos and getting involved in permissive sexual behavior.[5] watching MTV, adolescents' attitudes were reported to be more accepting of premarital sex.[6]

American youth in general listen to music about two hours per day. A study performed with a small sample of at-risk youth revealed an average of almost seven hours of music listening per day.[7]

Lyrics have become more explicit in their references to drugs, sex, and violence over the years.[8]

The bottom line when it comes to music: Be careful little ears what you hear!

My child, pay attention to what I say.

Listen carefully to my words.

Don't lose sight of them.

Let them penetrate deep into your heart,
for they bring life to those who find them,
    and healing to their whole body.
Guard your heart above all else,
    for it determines the course of your life.
Avoid all perverse talk;
    stay away from corrupt speech.
Look straight ahead,
    and fix your eyes on what lies before you.
Mark out a straight path for your feet;
    stay on the safe path.
Don't get sidetracked;
    keep your feet from following evil
    (Prov. 4:20-27 NLT).

The World's Fashion

How do you determine what clothes are acceptable to wear? Do you base your decisions on the latest styles? On what looks flattering on you? On what's available in the stores?

There's nothing wrong with looking nice, and I believe God is pleased when we take care of ourselves.

God's Word says, "Women should adorn themselves in respectable apparel, with modesty and self-control" (1 Tim. 2:9). The verse actually says that women *should* adorn themselves. The question then is how.

The danger for a woman, in particular, is dressing to please men rather than dressing to please God. Paul tells us,

Do you not know that your body is a temple
of the Holy Spirit within you, whom you have
from God? You are not your own, for you were

bought with a price. So glorify God in your body (1 Cor. 6:19-20).

Here's a definition for modesty:

> *Modesty* is a mode of dress and deportment intended to avoid encouraging sexual attraction in others; actual standards vary widely. In this use, it can be considered inappropriate or immodest to reveal certain parts of the body. A modest person would behave so as to avoid encouraging the sexual attention of others.[9]

We're living in a selfie generation where preoccupation with self has been normalized. But the Scottish preacher Robert Murray McCheyne said, "For every look at self, take ten looks at Christ! Live near to Jesus—and all things will appear little to you in comparison with eternal realities."[10]

God's Word gives instruction to women on where their focus should be:

> I want women to be modest in their appearance. They should wear decent and appropriate clothing and not draw attention to themselves by the way they fix their hair or by wearing gold or pearls or expensive clothes. For women who claim to be devoted to God should make themselves attractive by the good things they do (1 Tim. 2:9-10 NLT).

> Don't be concerned about the outward beauty of fancy hairstyles, expensive jewelry, or beautiful clothes. You should clothe yourselves instead with the beauty that comes from within, the unfading beauty of a gentle and quiet spirit, which is so precious to God (1 Peter 3:3-4 NLT).

> Charm is deceitful, and beauty is vain, but a woman who fears the Lord is to be praised (Prov. 31:30).

These verses clearly show us the source of true beauty. It's not what you put on that makes you beautiful, but rather what is within.

No doubt you've come across people who are considered beautiful by the world's standards, but who don't seem beautiful to you because of their unpleasant character. Conversely, others who are generally considered plain or unattractive may appear beautiful to you because of the "hidden person of the heart" (1 Peter 3:4).

I've never forgotten my mother's wise words when I was young, words that were likely spoken after someone had complimented me on my appearance. My mother told me, "The compliments of greatest value are those that have to do with character, because your character is something you have control over."

Our physical appearance is how God made us; therefore, we can't take credit for it. Our character, however, is something we develop and have control over.

Do Not Love the World

During the early years after my husband professed faith in Christ, he found himself still drawn away from the Lord by the things of this world. In his own words, Brad says, "I was like a lightbulb that was plugged in but not turned on."

Brad was a university student at the time and was living the party lifestyle. His mother would call him weekly and each time encourage him to contact the leader of the Christian club on campus, the Navigators. Brad set out several times to go to a Navigators meeting, but then turned back. Finally, he made it to one of their meetings.

From that day onward, he began to get into God's Word and to fellowship with other believers. He didn't think he could have fun without drinking, but he says, "During that year, I had the best time of my life."

"Do not love the world or the things in the world. If anyone loves the world, the love of the Father is not in him" (1 John 2:15). This is the exhortation given to those who desire to follow Jesus.

Entertainment, money, music, and fashion are all part of the world's system. They're not evil in and of themselves, but they all have the potential to draw a person away from the one who's worthy of our undivided affection—the Lord Jesus Christ. We must be diligent to examine ourselves regularly to see where our affections lie.

If you think having Jesus as the primary object of our affection while forsaking other loves will lead to a boring life, I assure you this isn't true.

Jesus exhorted us with these words: "Seek the Kingdom of God above all else, and live righteously, and he will give you everything you need" (Matt. 6:33 NLT). We don't need to worry about money, clothing, or possessions.

Living a holy life should be the goal of all true believers in the Lord Jesus. If, however, living a holy life isn't something you're striving for, I strongly encourage you to examine yourself to see if you're in the faith.

Please note that I didn't say a Christian must be perfectly holy; the key word is striving. At the moment of salvation, a person is born again and justified in the eyes of God. Justification in the biblical sense is the declaring of a person to be just or righteous before God. It's a legal term signifying acquittal. Sanctification is the ongoing process of growing in holiness to become more like Christ. This is the goal of all true believers. We struggle, we fail, and we continue to try with the strength that God gives us.

John Piper said, "The mark of a believer is not the absence of sin but the fact that we are fighting sin."[11]

REMEMBER

The things you cherish and invest your time in are greater indicators of what you love than what you say you love.

Ask Yourself

1. What should be our standard in viewing entertainment and listening to music?

2. Is there an area of your life in which you have a hard time doing the right thing when no one's looking?

3. What should determine how we dress?

4. What does Scripture tell us about loving the world?

5. What gives you the most joy in your life?

CHAPTER ELEVEN

Dying to Self

Whoever wants to be my disciple must deny themselves
and take up their cross and follow me.
Mark 8:34 NIV

J esus said, "Whoever does not carry their cross and
follow me cannot be my disciple" (Luke 14:27 NIV).
Did he really mean that we cannot be his disciples unless
we carry our cross and follow him? It's easy to gloss over
passages like this. By doing so, in essence, we're saying that
Jesus didn't really mean what he said.

What does it mean to take up your cross? Let's start
by explaining what it does not mean. Often you hear
people talk of the difficulties in their lives, then end the
conversation by saying, "Well, I guess it's just the cross I
have to bear." That's absolutely not what Jesus meant when
he said Christians must carry their cross.

The cross is a symbol of death. In Jesus' day, the
Romans would force convicted criminals to carry their
own cross to the place of crucifixion. As they bore their
cross, there would typically be people hurling abuse and
insults at them. This was the expectation of one who bore
a cross: insults, shame, humiliation, and ultimately death.

When Jesus said you need to carry your cross, he meant
you need to be prepared to die—die to yourself, and in
some cases even physical death.

Dietrich Bonhoeffer is often quoted as saying, "When Christ calls a man, he bids him come and die." Here's the context for that quote:

> The cross is laid on every Christian. The first Christ-suffering which every man must experience is the call to abandon the attachments of this world. It is that dying of the old man which is the result of his encounter with Christ. As we embark upon discipleship we surrender ourselves to Christ in union with his death—we give over our lives to death. Thus it begins; the cross is not the terrible end to an otherwise God-fearing and happy life, but it meets us at the beginning of our communion with Christ. *When Christ calls a man, he bids him come and die.* It may be a death like that of the first disciples who had to leave home and work to follow him, or it may be a death like Luther's, who had to leave the monastery and go out into the world. But it is the same death every time—death in Jesus Christ, the death of the old man at his call.[1]

Being a Christian is not for the faint of heart. Either you carry your cross, die to self, and follow Jesus, or you're not a disciple. Jesus makes this clear in Luke 14:27.

The world's philosophy tells us to live for self; God's Word tells us to die to self:

> I have been crucified with Christ. It is no longer I who live, but Christ who lives in me. And the life I now live in the flesh I live by faith in the Son of God, who loved me and gave himself for me Gal. 2:20).

George Mueller, known for his great faith as he ministered to orphans in nineteenth-century England, was asked the secret of his service for God. He answered,

> There was a day when I died, utterly…died to George Muller, his opinions, preferences, tastes, and will—died to the world…died to the approval or blame of even my brethren and friends—and since then I have studied to show myself approved only unto God.[2]

Here's the paradox: To live, you must die. As Jesus said,

> Unless a grain of wheat falls into the earth and dies, it remains alone; but if it dies, it bears much fruit. Whoever loves his life loses it, and whoever hates his life in this world will keep it for eternal life (John 12:24-25).

For a seed to bear fruit, it first must die; there's no other way.

The apostle Paul continues the discussion of dying to self in his epistle to the Romans: "For we know that our old self was crucified with him so that the body ruled by sin might be done away with, that we should no longer be slaves to sin" (Rom. 6:6 NIV). Christians are no longer under the dominion of sin.

"When you produce much fruit," Jesus said, "you are my true disciples" (John 15:8 NLT). Do you see the connection? True disciples carry their cross, die to themselves, and live for Christ—and the result is fruit. You cannot bear spiritual fruit unless you first die. Dying to self and bearing fruit go hand-in-hand. You can't have one without the other. Both are marks of a true follower of Jesus. Christians have died and continue to die to themselves. We're to take up our crosses daily.

The more we feed our desires, the more they grow. I experienced this in my own life recently after I taught my eldest son how to play chess. It started innocently enough with the two of us occasionally challenging one another to a game. I also found a website that allowed him to play with other people online. We were part of a homeschool co-op at the time, and I thought it would be fun to offer chess as one of the activities in the co-op. When I began playing chess online, I found I really enjoyed it, and my game also began to improve. Over time I found myself wanting to play more and more. In the evenings when I should have been going to bed, I would tell myself, "Just one more game."

That one game would often turn to two, then three. It became a bit of an obsession, so I realized I needed to set down some rules for myself. I determined to allow myself two games a day, which worked fine for a while.

One evening when my two games were done, I decided to play the next day's games, and the two games for the next night also. Before I knew it, hours had passed, and I was still playing.

I would slip off during the day to get a game in sometimes, and if anyone stepped into the room, my instinct was to switch the screen. I knew chess had become an obsession, and I was embarrassed by it.

There were many nights when I would play half the night, then slip into bed quietly, hoping my husband wouldn't awaken and look at the clock.

I tried to manage my obsession with different strategies. I wouldn't allow myself to play for a whole week. When the week was up, I was back at it the same as before.

I rationalized my behavior, telling myself that it wasn't

that big a deal since I didn't watch TV in the evenings as many people did, so this was okay for me.

The bottom line is—I had become an addict. What I was going through with chess is no different than what a porn addict experiences as he tries to hide his online activities. While there's nothing immoral or wrong about playing online chess, it reached the point where I knew I had to give it up, because it consumed my thoughts and ate up huge chunks of my time.

Finally, I made a New Year's resolution that I wouldn't play for a full year. I stuck with that decision, and as the year progressed, I missed it less and less.

For some, having a chess addiction may seem laughable, but I assure you it wasn't for me. Anything that has a grip on our lives is serious business and needs to be dealt with.

Dying to self looks different in each person's life, but if we want to be disciples of Jesus, we need to be willing to deal with whatever it is that consumes us.

The apostle Paul says, "For we know that our old self was crucified with him so that the body ruled by sin might be done away with, that we should no longer be slaves to sin" (Rom. 6:6 NIV). Christians are no longer under the dominion of sin. "Sin is no longer your master" (Rom. 6:14 NLT).

In *The Discipline of Grace,* Jerry Bridges writes,

> The question arises, however, "If we died to sin's dominion, why do we still struggle with sin in our daily lives?" When Paul wrote, "We died to sin; how can we live in it any longer?" he was referring not to the activity of committing sins, but to continuing to live under the dominion of sin. The word *live* means to continue in or

abide in. It connotes a settled course of life. To use Paul's words from Romans 8:7, "The sinful mind [one under sin's dominion] is hostile to God. It does not submit to God's law, nor can it do so." But the believer who has died to sin's reign and dominion delights in God's law. The believer approves of it as holy, righteous, and good (Rom. 7:12), even though he or she may struggle to obey it. We must distinguish between the activity of sin, which is true in all believers, and the dominion of sin, which is true of all unbelievers.[3]

Although Christians still sin, this is not the dominating force in their life.

———•———

Many would-be disciples turned away from following Jesus because the cost was too high. In Luke 9:57-62, we meet three men who had a desire to follow Jesus.

The first man came to Jesus, saying, "I will follow you wherever you go." Jesus said to him, "Foxes have holes, and birds of the air have nests, but the Son of Man has nowhere to lay his head."

Jesus wasn't very encouraging. Instead of welcoming this eager man into the fold, he slowed him down with a shot of reality, as if to say, "Do you know what you'd be signing up for? Following me will cost you the comforts of this life."

The second man said to Jesus, "Lord, let me first go and bury my father." Jesus responded, "Leave the dead to bury their own dead. But as for you, go and proclaim the kingdom of God."

There are a couple of possibilities for the meaning of this verse. I'll mention just one. Some suggest that this man's father wasn't yet dead. In that case, what he was saying was this: I need to be home to take care of my father; once he's dead, I'll be free to follow you. Jesus emphasizes to this man the superiority of spiritual priorities.

This is consistent with his teaching in Matthew 10:37: "Whoever loves father or mother more than me is not worthy of me, and whoever loves son or daughter more than me is not worthy of me."

Proclaiming the kingdom of God must be the highest priority, even above family. This teaching is also applicable to the third man who wanted to say goodbye to his family. That doesn't seem an unreasonable request, yet Jesus said to him, "No one who puts his hand to the plow and looks back is fit for the kingdom of God" (Luke 9:62).

Jesus is clear. Our desires must take a back seat to his. Our relationship with him must be over and above any human relationship. "And whoever does not carry their cross and follow me cannot be my disciple" (Luke 14:27 NIV).

Perhaps you're thinking, *That's over the top! You don't need to do that to be a Christian.* If that's your sentiment, perhaps you should ask yourself: Did Jesus really mean what he said?

REMEMBER

The world's philosophy says, "Live for self." God's Word says, "Die to self."

Ask Yourself

1. In your own words, what does it mean to "take up your cross"?

2. What are Christians to die to?

3. Has there been a cost for you to follow Christ? If you are just now counting the cost, what will it be?

4. Is there an area of your life where it has been hard to die to self? Describe this.

5. Why must our relationship with Christ come first in our lives?

CHAPTER TWELVE

Those Who Counted the Cost

For it has been granted to you that for the sake of Christ you should not only believe in him but also suffer for his sake.
Philippians 1:29

The updated *Foxe's Book of Martyrs* tells stories of those who counted the cost. Here are two:

> For refusing to stop preaching about Christ, evangelist Ni-Tio-Sen had his eyes gouged out, and his tongue and both hands cut off. He was then sent to a prison in Shanghai, China.[1]

> Franco Gjini of Albania was kept in a nine-foot by nine-foot concrete cell for sixty-eight days. Several times pieces of wood were driven under his fingernails. Toward the end, he was given electric shocks. Then he was shot. As he went to the place of his execution, he encouraged other prisoners to stay strong in their faith.[2]

Richard Wurmbrand tells how a certain pastor was tortured for his faith in Christ:

> A pastor by the name of Florescu was tortured with red-hot pokers and knives. He was beaten very badly. Then starving rats were driven into

his cell through a large pipe. He could not sleep, but had to defend himself all the time. If he rested a moment, the rats would attack him.

He was forced to stand for two weeks, day and night. The Communists wished to compel him to betray his brethren, but he resisted steadfastly. In the end, they brought in his fourteen-year-old son and began to whip the boy in front of his father, saying they would continue to beat him until the pastor said what they wished him to say. The poor man was half mad. He bore it as long as he could.

When he could not stand it anymore, he cried to his son: "Alexander, I must say what they want! I can't bear your beating anymore!"

The son answered, "Father, don't do me the injustice to have a traitor as a parent. Withstand! If they kill me, I will die with the words, 'Jesus and my fatherland.'"

The Communists, enraged, fell upon the child and beat him to death, with blood spattered over the walls of the cell. He died praising God. Our dear brother Florescu was never the same after seeing this.[3]

History is replete with the accounts of faithful Christians who've suffered for Jesus, including millions who've paid the ultimate price. Referencing such martyrs, Paul Washer made the following statement in a sermon:

Isn't it amazing that we're going to have believers from China, believers from Northern Nigeria that have died as martyrs, dragged through the desert behind camels, some of them skinned alive, but they would not deny Jesus. And here's all these American Christians standing beside them that couldn't even find enough of anything inside them to even attend church on Sunday morning. Does anybody have a problem with that? One man can be skinned alive and not deny Christ, and the other denies him in the smallest of things. And yet, they're all born again? I think not, my friend. I think not.[4]

Amy Carmichael, who spent most of her life as a missionary in Bangalore, India, is someone I've admired since I was a teenager. She wrote many books, as well as poetry. One of her poems, "No Scar," I find particularly impactful:

Hast thou no scar?
    No hidden scar on foot, or side, or hand?
I hear thee sung as mighty in the land,
    I hear them hail thy bright ascendant star,
Hast thou no scar?
    Hast thou no wound?
Yet I was wounded by the archers, spent,
    Leaned Me against a tree to die, and rent
    by ravening beasts that compassed Me, I
    swooned:
Hast thou no wound?
    No wound, no scar?
Yet as the Master shall the servant be,
    And, pierced are the feet that follow Me;
But thine are whole: can he have followed far
    Who has no wound nor scar?[5]

While most of us will not be tortured for our faith, there is still a price to be paid. The life of Rosaria Butterfield illustrates that point. Before God got hold of her life, she was a tenured professor of English and women's studies at Syracuse University. Her primary academic field was critical theory, specializing in queer theory. She was a lesbian activist with a low opinion of Christians, whom she considered "bad thinkers."

In 1997, while Rosaria was researching the Religious Right and, in her words, "their politics of hatred against people like me," she wrote an editorial that elicited so much hate mail and fan mail that she separated the letters into two boxes.

She received one letter, however, that didn't fit into either of those categories. It was from a local pastor named Ken Smith. The letter was kind and inquiring, encouraging her to explore the kind of questions she admired: "How did you arrive at your interpretations? How do you know you are right?"

He didn't argue with Rosaria but rather asked her to defend her presuppositions.

She didn't know which box to put the pastor's letter in, so it sat on her desk for a week until, finally, she called him. After a pleasant conversation, he invited Rosaria to talk further with him over a home-cooked meal prepared by his wife, Floy.

Rosaria accepted the offer, since she was interested in continuing their discussion. She also accepted out of curiosity. She "was excited to meet a real born-again Christian and find out why he believed such silly ideas." She considered getting together with Ken and Floy part of her research.

Before the meal, Ken prayed an unpretentious prayer. Ken and Floy didn't fit her stereotypical idea of Christians. During the meal, she kept waiting to be "punched in the stomach with something grossly offensive." That moment never happened.

At that time, Rosaria believed that God was dead—or if he was ever alive, the facts of poverty, racism, homophobia, and war proved that he didn't care. But Ken's faith seemed alive.

They freely conversed on many topics that evening. Rosaria noted that "Ken and Floy didn't identify with me. They listened to me and identified with Christ."

For two years, Rosaria met with Ken and Floy, getting to know them and studying Scripture.

After they had been meeting for a while, Pastor Ken asked if he could speak to her English majors about why the Bible is a foundational book for English majors to read. She wasn't comfortable with that idea, so she asked if he would be willing to present the lecture to an audience of one—her. He agreed.

During the lecture, Ken gave an overview of all sixty-six books of the Bible with a focus on redemption. She was both intrigued and infuriated because if what Ken said was true, then everything she believed was false.

After two years of private meetings, she attended church for the first time. She felt like a freak in the church but was drawn to keep going back.

I'll share what happened next in her own words:

> I prayed and asked God if the gospel message was for someone like me too. I prayed that if Jesus was truly a real and risen God, that he would change my heart. And if he was real and

if I was his, I prayed that he would give me the strength of mind to follow him and the character to become a godly woman. I prayed for the strength of character to repent for a sin that at that time didn't feel like sin at all— it felt like life, plain and simple. I prayed that if my life was actually his life, that he would take it back and make it what he wanted it to be. I asked him to take it all: my sexuality, my profession, my community, my tastes, my books, and my tomorrows.

Two worldviews clashed: the reality of my lived experience and the truth of the word of God.[6]

Rosaria understood what so many fail to grasp: There's a cost to following Jesus.

She struggled to find answers to her questions. How could she and everyone she knew and loved be in sin? What did Christians do with their past? How did they let go of their past without losing their identity? She wondered who she would be without her lesbian identity.

For two years she wrestled with the Bible, reading it as she was trained to read other books. She examined its textual authority, authorship, canonicity, and internal hermeneutics. As she devoured its pages, slowly over time, the Bible started to take on a life and a meaning she didn't anticipate. This wasn't just another book, but one inspired by a holy God.

One pastor told her that she could have Jesus and her lesbian lover. As convenient as that would have been, she knew her Bible and chose to submit to the authority of God's Word rather than the opinions of man.

Despite her struggles over these hard questions,

Rosaria finally surrendered her life to the Lord, realizing that repentance requires that we draw near to Jesus no matter what.

When Christ gave her the strength to follow him, Rosaria said she didn't stop feeling like a lesbian. She discovered that the Lord doesn't change our feelings until we obey him.

That reminds me of the advice I was given many years ago by Ken Fleming, my missions professor at Emmaus Bible College. I was trying to decide where I should go as a missionary. I wanted to hear God's voice before making a move. He told me that God couldn't steer a stationary vehicle; you must first get into gear. Step out in faith, then God can direct.

In the same way, Rosaria stepped out in faith on the authority of the Word of God. She agreed with God about what he calls sin, and in repentance she moved toward the Lord and away from self.

Many people tend to classify sin, yet in God's eyes, sin is sin. The same list of sin that includes homosexuality also includes gossip and disobedience to parents. Heterosexual sin is as offensive to a holy God as is homosexual sin.

Rosaria Butterfield says, "Repentance requires greater intimacy with God than with our sin. How much greater? About the size of a mustard seed."[7]

There's a cost to following Jesus. In Rosaria Butterfield's own words: "I lost everything but the dog." She lost her job, many friends, and a community she loved.

The cost isn't the same for everyone, but for everyone, there is a cost.

Jesus told the crowds they needed to be willing to carry

their own cross if they wanted to be his disciples. Then he launched into this:

> Which of you, desiring to build a tower, does not first sit down and count the cost, whether he has enough to complete it? Otherwise, when he has laid a foundation and is not able to finish, all who see it begin to mock him, saying, 'This man began to build and was not able to finish.' Or what king, going out to encounter another king in war, will not sit down first and deliberate whether he is able with ten thousand to meet him who comes against him with twenty thousand? And if not, while the other is yet a great way off, he sends a delegation and asks for terms of peace. So therefore, any one of you who does not renounce all that he has cannot be my disciple (Luke 14:28-33).

In other words, Jesus is saying, "You need to think this through."

The lives of great men and women who've gone before us can inspire us. There's more to becoming a Christian than signing a commitment card or repeating a prayer.

REMEMBER

Being a Christian is a total life commitment.

Ask Yourself

1. What price have you paid—or are you willing to pay—for following Jesus?

2. What if following Jesus results in you losing your friends? Would you still follow Jesus?

3. What if following Jesus costs you your job? Would you still follow Jesus?

4. What if your family disowns you? Would you still follow Jesus?

5. What if following Jesus means losing your life? Would you still be willing to follow?

CHAPTER THIRTEEN

The Gospel of Greed

*For the love of money
is a root of all kinds of evils.*
1 Timothy 6:10

If you were to make a list of things that you think would keep people out of heaven, greed would probably not be at the top. Yet greed is mentioned in every list in the Bible that describes people who will not inherit the kingdom of God. In fact, greed and sexual immorality are tied for first place in how often they're stated as things that will keep you out of heaven.[1]

The world has always had its share of greedy people, and there are even those who make a living off greed in the name of Jesus. I'm referring to prosperity preachers who lure people with the promise of material blessings and physical healing.

I recently read a scathing comment about the prosperity gospel from an unlikely source. Costi Hinn, the nephew of televangelist Benny Hinn, said this: "The prosperity gospel is damning and abusive. It exploits the poor and ruins the lives of some of the world's most vulnerable people."[2]

Costi grew up believing that if he asked for anything in Jesus' name, he would receive it. For him, it was as simple as that, since it seemed to be working for his family.

His Uncle Benny told people that the way to receive a miracle for sickness and disease was to give their money to God. He would say, "No money? No miracle!"[3] God's favor in a person's life was proportionate to their giving. Giving was the key to God's divine bank account.

A hero of Benny Hinn's was Oral Roberts, another televangelist and founder of Oral Roberts University in Tulsa, Oklahoma. In January of 1987, Roberts said that God would call him home if he didn't receive eight million dollars from donors to fund the building of a hospital by March 31.[4] The money came in, and Roberts went on to say that he would need that amount of money every year until Jesus returns.[5]

In his book on the life of Oral Roberts, Edwin Harrell Jr. writes, "Millions of people throughout the world consider Oral Roberts a prophet of God. Millions more believe him to be a charlatan."[6]

Costi Hinn grew up in this name-it-and-claim-it environment. His father had his own ministry, but he also worked for his brother Benny. Money poured in, and the family lived the life of luxury, with mansions in both British Columbia and California. They ate in the fanciest restaurants, wore fine clothes, and gave themselves whatever their hearts desired.

Costi, too, joined the ministry and began traveling the world and enjoying all the perks that went along with it. Over time some of the methods of solicitation began to bother him. One night during an appeal for money, Costi began to feel the conviction of the Holy Spirit. When he questioned his father, Costi was silenced.

On a trip to Mumbai, India, at the age of nineteen, he came face-to-face with despair as he'd never seen before.

He noticed people sitting in gutters and children playing in filth. It caused his stomach to churn as he thought of his luxury hotel.

His heart began softening, and he finally realized he existed to glorify God, not himself. He cried about things he'd never cried about before. He saw in his mind the faces of so many hurting people, and he felt broken over the part he'd played in exploiting them with false hope.

He repented of his sins, the false teaching, the hypocrisy, and the way he'd twisted the gospel for greedy gain. He asked the Lord for forgiveness and a fresh start. Costi committed to studying, teaching, and standing up for the truth no matter the cost. He was willing to do whatever it took to make things right.

Even before that day, Costi had begun to count the cost of following the true Jesus. Costi went from driving a Hummer to driving an economy car, from having nearly ten thousand square feet of living space to having only six hundred, from sleeping in a luxury bed to sleeping on a mattress on the floor, and from an exorbitant salary to a job paying ten dollars per hour.

Some people may have considered Costi a failure, but he felt as though he'd hit the jackpot—he had peace and could sleep guilt-free at night.

Although it was hard at first, Costi knew that he'd found the truth—and the truth had set him free.

<hr/>

In Paul's letter to Timothy, he speaks of people who are teaching a "different doctrine." He describes these people as "depraved in mind and deprived of the truth, imagining that godliness is a means of gain" (1 Tim. 6:5). Paul goes on to explain what the attitude of the Christian should be and to give a warning.

> But godliness with contentment is great gain, for we brought nothing into the world, and we cannot take anything out of the world. But if we have food and clothing, with these we will be content. But those who desire to be rich fall into temptation, into a snare, into many senseless and harmful desires that plunge people into ruin and destruction. For the love of money is a root of all kinds of evils. It is through this craving that some have wandered away from the faith and pierced themselves with many pangs (1 Tim. 6:6-8).

In *God, Greed, and the Prosperity Gospel*, Costi Hinn writes:

> The prosperity gospel appeals to the deep longing of every human heart for peace, health, wealth, and happiness. There is nothing wrong with wanting a good and happy life, but the prosperity gospel uses Jesus Christ as a pawn in its get-rich-quick scam. The prosperity gospel sells salvation and false hope. But true and lasting peace can be found only through faith in the Lord Jesus Christ.[7]

This false hope was dished out to Larry and Darcy Fardette, who believed televangelist Todd Coontz when he asked his viewers to write him a check for $273 as an "investment in their faith and future." The appeal was made as a "seed-faith offering" accompanied by such verbiage as this: "Send me a hundred dollars and trust God to give you back a thousand."

Over the years, the Fardettes had already given about twenty thousand dollars to Coontz and various other ministries, and this time as well Larry sent the amount specified by Coontz. Larry had the impression the money would be given for worthy causes at home and abroad. He also believed help would be there for him if he ever found himself in a desperate situation.

The day came when Larry wasn't well and his daughter was seriously ill and needed costly treatment. The seed-faith money he'd planted had not multiplied, so he needed help. He appealed in a five-page letter to several ministries he'd contributed to over the years, saying, "As a father, I am presently helpless.... Would you please consider sponsorship to save our daughter's life?"

None of the ministries he appealed to sent help. "We had been faithful to these ministries," Larry said. "They called us partners, friends, family. We thought they'd be there for us." The Fardettes exhausted all their funds and eventually became homeless. After seeing an exposé of prosperity preachers, the Fardettes did some investigating and today are free from this type of spiritual manipulation. They say a veil has been lifted from their eyes.[8]

Many are able to see through these wolves in sheep's clothing. Sadly, others are blinded by the promise of a blessing which will lead them out of poverty, and they suffer terribly as a result.

While donors sacrifice their finances to these ministries, some televangelists live unapologetically luxurious life-styles. Private jets are commonplace among them.

In March 2015, televangelist Creflo Dollar, the founder of World Changers Church International, began fundraising for a new ministry aircraft. He called it the

Project G650 Campaign and hoped to get 200,000 people to donate $399 each so his ministry could buy a brand-new luxurious Gulfstream G650 jet priced at sixty-five million dollars. Billionaires were reportedly on a wait list for this plane. But after a public outcry, the crowdfunding campaign ended. Even though they ended the fundraiser, the church still managed to get the plane. They claimed it was necessary for ministry.[9]

In 2018, New Orleans televangelist Jesse Duplantis claimed that God told him, "I want you to believe me for a Falcon 7-X"—a jet valued at fifty-four million dollars.[10] A piece by *Inside Edition* called "Living Lavish" includes a clip of Jesse Duplantis saying, "One of my chandeliers costs more than most people's houses; I've got twenty-two chandeliers."[11]

Another jetsetter is televangelist Kenneth Copeland, who owns two private jets and has his own airport located next to his mansion.

The false hope of the prosperity gospel was promoted to eager audiences by Oral Roberts throughout his lifetime, enabling him to become a very rich man. In a biography of Roberts, author Edwin Harrell Jr. writes, "In addition to his healthy income, derived mostly from book royalties, Oral continued to enjoy generous expense accounts."[12] Roberts and his wife wore expensive clothes and jewelry and traveled in a company-owned eight-passenger fanjet. Within his lifetime, Oral Roberts wrote seventy books from which he received hefty royalties.

John Piper has also written more than seventy books. One significant difference between these two men is that John Piper gives away the royalty payments for his books. Piper explained why he does this in an interview in 2016.

Like everybody else, I get a wage for what I do, and I don't need those royalties.... It's dangerous to be rich. Jesus said it's hard for a rich person to get into the kingdom of heaven; he said those who desire to be rich stumble into all kinds of desires that pierce the soul. He said, "It's more blessed to give than to receive." He said, "Freely you've received, freely give." Everything that I admire in the Bible about Jesus and everything that I look at by way of danger disinclines me to want to take these royalties, because there's a lot of them. I don't want to be rich.[13]

To deal with the book income, John Piper and his wife created the Desiring God Foundation. It's run by a board whose charge is to own and protect the copyrights and to take the royalties and channel them into ministry. Riches themselves are not evil, but John Piper has safeguarded himself against becoming ensnared by riches.

Costi Hinn says in his book:

In an effort to operate with transparency and integrity, allow me to state the obvious: a book speaking against the prosperity gospel technically makes money off of the prosperity gospel. As such it is my conviction that a word concerning the use of royalties is appropriate here. I intend to use proceeds from this book to fund theological education and resources for pastors and leaders who have been exploited by the prosperity gospel. I pray that this project will give more than it ever takes. May it be blessed to be a blessing.[14]

The point of these examples is not about keeping or not keeping a royalty check, since this is not an issue for most people. Wealth is not evil. The issue here, as with other areas in life, is the heart. God sees our hearts, and we must guard our hearts against greed.

Greed is defined as "intense and selfish desire for something, especially wealth, power, or food."[15]

God tells us, "For of this you can be sure: No immoral, impure or greedy person—such a person is an idolater—has any inheritance in the kingdom of Christ and of God" (Eph. 5:5 NIV). These are God's words, not mine. If greed is the pattern of your life, you will not enter the kingdom of God. It's a test of true faith. That's not to say I'm disqualified from heaven if I do a greedy act. What it means is that if I'm habitually greedy, this is evidence that I don't have the Spirit of God. God and greed cannot coexist.

Prosperity preachers will stand before God and give account for what they've done and taught, but the problem of greed is not confined to the rich and famous. We, too, will stand before God and give account for our own lives. It's easy to point a finger at public and corporate greed, but what about the greed in my life and yours? Even as I've been writing this chapter, God has revealed to me areas in my life where I've been guilty of greed. I've confessed those sins and am so thankful for his forgiveness.

Paul tells us we're to "flee these things. Pursue righteousness, godliness, faith, love, steadfastness, gentleness" (1 Tim. 6:11). He then goes on to say that we're to "do good, to be rich in good works, to be generous and ready to share" (1 Tim. 6:18).

What you pursue in this life reveals who you really are—but more importantly, it reveals whose you are. My prayer for you and for myself is that godliness would be the goal.

REMEMBER

In the Bible, greed is mentioned in every list of people who will not inherit the kingdom of God.

Ask Yourself

1. How high on your priority list is making money?

2. What priorities in your life would cause people to consider you a greedy person?

3. In what ways has the love of money affected your relationships with others?

4. Do you agree that stinginess is a form of greed? Why or why not?

5. In your life, what do you do—or what can you do—to avoid being ensnared by a desire for wealth?

CHAPTER FOURTEEN

The Gospel of Self

In the last days there will come times of difficulty.
For people will be lovers of self, lovers of money, proud,
arrogant... lovers of pleasure rather than lovers of God.
2 Timothy 3:1-4

Some would consider Joel Osteen (pastor of Lakewood Church in Houston, Texas) to be the poster boy for the gospel of self, while others have no problem with his message. Before researching this chapter, I wasn't quite sure what to think.

What's wrong with encouraging people by saying things like the following?

> If you are always talking about your problems, don't be surprised if you are living in perpetual defeat.[1]

> Quit comparing your life to somebody else's, and quit dwelling on what could have been, should have been, or might have been.[2]

I bought Joel Osteen's book *Your Best Life Now* (which has sold five million copies) so I could discover the truth for myself and not base my opinions on what other people say or from quotes without context.

Osteen's church is one of the largest in America.[3] His sermons are televised and seen by over seven million people weekly in more than a hundred countries.[4] The apostle Paul set a biblical standard for Christian teachers when he exhorted both Titus and Timothy to teach sound doctrine. With so many people looking to Joel Osteen for spiritual advice, I think it's a reasonable expectation that he teach sound doctrine. But does he?

After reading *Your Best Life Now,* here's what I've found.

When I searched the Kindle book for expressions that seemed to appear frequently, my suspicion was confirmed. The expression "God wants" is used ninety-seven times. Eighty-six of those times, it refers to what God wants to do for you. I put that firmly in the category of self. Here is a representative sampling:[5]

- "God wants you to accomplish great things in life."
- "God wants to bless you."
- "God wants to use us in spite of your weaknesses."
- "God wants you to be a winner, not a whiner."
- "God wants to increase you financially, by giving you promotions, fresh ideas, and creativity."
- "God wants to do a new thing in your life. Don't limit him with your small thinking."

Eight times the book refers to what God wants you to do for someone else—for others beside yourself. Some examples:[6]

- "God wants us to build people up."
- "God wants to use you to bring hope, healing, love, and victory to people wherever you go."

There were two mentions of what God wants that I wasn't sure how to categorize. One said, "Be sensitive and obedient to what God wants you to do."[7] That statement was in the context of showing compassion, so I decided to place it in the category of what God wants us to do for someone else. That now makes nine times that others are mentioned in connection with what God wants.

That left me with one final reference to what God wants: "God wants us to be people of excellence and integrity."[8]

I thought, *At least one refers to our character in relation to God.* I then read it again in context and saw this line immediately following: "If you don't have integrity, you will never reach your highest potential. Integrity is the foundation on which a truly successful life is built."[9] With integrity framed in this what's-in-it-for-me context, I placed it in the larger category of self, bringing the total there to eighty-eight, compared to nine references to what God wants me to do for others.

Do you notice a glaring omission from a list of what God wants? As a child, I learned this acronym for the word *joy*:

J—Jesus
O—Others
Y—Yourself

What should be number one hasn't even made Osteen's list. Although I was anticipating a strong emphasis on self, I still found this surprising.

According to the Bible, some of the things God wants you to do are:

- Repent (2 Peter 3:9).
- Be holy (1 Thes. 4:3).
- Abstain from sexual immorality (1 Thes. 4:3).
- Love him with all your heart, soul, and mind (Mark 12:30-31).

- Love your neighbor as yourself (Mark 12:30-31).
- Do nothing out of selfish ambition or vain conceit (Phil. 2:3).

The Bible is clear that the goal for a Christian is not self-exaltation, but rather self-denial (Matt. 16:24).

Paula White—a televangelist and prosperity gospel preacher—disagrees. At a women's convention in Orlando, Florida, she reportedly said, "Anyone who tells you to deny yourself is from Satan."[10]

Sin and repentance are not popular topics at Lakewood Church or other churches with the same philosophy.

In a message titled "False Faith," Alistair Begg (pastor of Cleveland's Parkside Church) quotes the teaching of Thomas Manton, an English Puritan. Though Manton was born four centuries ago, his words are surprisingly relevant to this topic of exalting self. Manton speaks of those who come to church "to repeat words because others do the same, to hear what is delivered from the pulpit with little attention or affection, unless something occurs that is suited to exalt self or to soothe conscience—and then to run with eagerness back out the door and into the world again." Begg comments on Manton's teaching:

> It's amazingly up to date, isn't it? Here he is, hundreds of years before, saying, "The thing that I'm facing in my congregation is this, that I have a vast crowd of people who come; many of them listen with very little attention and very little affection." The only way you can get them to listen, he says, is if you will exalt their self-esteem, or if you will seek to soothe their conscience—in other words,

in twenty-first-century terms, if you will tell them that they are great, and if you will tell them that they are okay. Why are there arenas this morning in the continental United States with thirty thousand people in them listening to preaching? I'll tell you why. Because the preaching says two things over and over again: You are great, and you are okay.[11]

This is the type of preaching heard from the pulpit of Joel Osteen. The problem with that type of preaching is that it isn't true. Jesus didn't come to save us from low self-esteem and a bad attitude; he came to save us from the consequence of our sin, which is death. We're not okay. Our situation is hopeless, and we're utterly helpless to save ourselves. No pep talk in the world is going to change that.

In a message called "Winning the Battle Every Time—Fulfilling Your Dominion Mandate," prosperity preacher Bill Winston said this:

You will persevere, you will win, you will come out on top. Every battle you will win, I declare in Jesus' name…. Whatever battle you are fighting, whether it is something healthwise or whatever, you are going to come out on top. Say amen to that.[12]

While this sounds good and makes the listeners feel good, the Bible clearly tells us life doesn't always work that way in this sin-cursed world. The apostle Paul was beaten, stoned, and shipwrecked; he suffered from a physical ailment, and he was ultimately killed for his faith. Paul might beg to differ with Bill Winston's rosy picture of the Christian life. In his letter to Timothy, Paul wrote, "All who desire to live a godly life in Christ Jesus will be persecuted" (2 Tim. 3:12). Notice that he says *all*, not some. Persecution is guaranteed if we desire to live godly lives.

In 2016, Joel Osteen was featured on CBS's *Sunday Morning* program. Reporter Tracy Smith opened the interview by saying, "You've been criticized for church-lite or a cotton-candy message. Do you feel like you're cheating people by not telling them about the hell part? Or repentance part?" Osteen responded by saying,

> No, I really don't, because it's a different approach.... [People] already feel guilty enough. They're not doing what they should, raising their kids—we can all find reasons. So I want them to come to Lakewood or our meetings and be lifted up, to say, "You know what? I may not be perfect, but I'm moving forward. I'm doing better." And I think that motivates you to do better.[13]

The apostle Paul gave this warning to Timothy (and to us all):

> A time is coming when people will not endure sound teaching, but having itching ears they will accumulate for themselves teachers to suit their own passions and will turn away from listening to the truth and wander off into myths (2 Tim. 4:3-4).

Victoria Osteen, co-pastor with her husband, addressed their congregation with these words:

> I just want to encourage every one of us to realize: When we obey God, we're not doing it for God. I mean, that's one way to look at it. We're doing it for ourselves. Because God takes pleasure when we're happy. That's the thing

that gives him the greatest joy this morning. So I want you to know this morning: Just do good for your own self. Do good, 'cause God wants you to be happy. When you come to church, when you worship him, you're not doing it for God, really. You're doing it for yourself, because that's what makes God happy. Amen?[14]

Wow! The messages from Joel and Victoria Osteen are usually a bit more subtle. This message, on the other hand, is so overtly contrary to Scripture that it would be difficult to hide that fact. If I hadn't heard her say these words myself via a YouTube video, I might have had a hard time believing she would say that.

What does all this mean? I opened the chapter by asking whether Joel Osteen teaches sound doctrine. I haven't singled out Osteen because I dislike him. In fact, he seems to genuinely believe what he's saying. My question, however, is not about his intentions. After reading his book and doing some research, I've concluded that he, in fact, does not teach sound doctrine. It isn't an insignificant matter of style but of substance. The true gospel is being distorted.

Paul, writing to the Galatians, said this:

> I am astonished that you are so quickly deserting him who called you in the grace of Christ and are turning to a different gospel—not that there is another one, but there are some who trouble you and want to distort the gospel of Christ. But even if we or an angel from heaven should preach to you a gospel contrary to the one we preached to you, let him be accursed. As we have said before, so now I say again: If

anyone is preaching to you a gospel contrary
to the one you received, let him be accursed
(Gal. 1:6-9).

Those are strong words, and my natural tendency is to shy away from coming on too strong. But just as I must speak the gospel as it is written, I also must speak God's condemnation of those who distort the gospel.

Joel Osteen is preaching a "me-centered gospel," and he's not alone. God's Word tells us to seek first the kingdom of God and his righteousness. You can't do both.

What's the harm? you might think. Couldn't we all use a little more positivity in this life?

But the harm comes in the fact that Joel Osteen is supposed to be a minister of the gospel. If he marketed himself as a motivational speaker or a life coach, there wouldn't be a problem with him encouraging people to stop focusing on their problems. But the fact is that people are looking to him—as a minister of the gospel—for answers to questions that are bigger than how to be happy in this life. People come looking for answers to questions such as how to have hope for the next life.

It's no small matter if people are being led astray.

My mother knew an East Indian man who'd become a Christian while in prison. He told her his Hindu brother liked listening to Joel Osteen.

The Muslim Times published an article in which they encouraged their readers to listen to Osteen's messages by saying, "He has no less than a thousand half-hour wonderful presentations about positive thinking, hope, optimism, and success."[15] The reason people of other faiths can comfortably listen to Osteen's messages is that he fails to preach the true gospel.

In an article headlined "Why is Joel Osteen considered a false teacher?" Evan Plante of Mainsail Ministries writes,

> Osteen's books answer the question, what must I do to become a better me? The Bible answers the question, what must I do to be saved? (Acts 16:30). In light of the latter, the former loses all importance.[16]

Jesus says, "For what will it profit a man if he gains the whole world and forfeits his soul? Or what shall a man give in return for his soul?" (Matt. 16:26).

In an inspirational video short entitled "Resurrection Power at Work" from Osteen's *Today's Word* website, he tells us we have reasons to celebrate because God is alive and is filled with resurrection power, and he wants to extend this resurrection power to us:

> Maybe you have a dream to get out of debt, pay off your house, or be free from that burden of lack, but it looks like it's impossible in the natural. Business is slow. The economy is down; you've gone as far as your education allows. But God is saying, "I'm not limited by those things, I've got resurrection power."… Your part is to keep believing today, knowing that he wants to bring you into supernatural increase.[17]

Did Jesus rise from the dead so I could have material blessings?

My father worked for the provincial government in Canada, starting in the 1950s as a photocopy operator, back when that was an actual position. Throughout his thirty-year career, he received many promotions, ultimately being named a director in the Ministry of Agriculture and Food.

Promotions were filled internally if there was a qualified applicant. If none was found, the position was advertised publicly. Before becoming a director, my dad interviewed for a position that he was qualified to fill, and he felt was a good opportunity. He was surprised to learn the job was filled outside the government. My father was naturally disappointed, but he felt the job would have been his if this had been God's will.

When he continued to fulfill his duties without complaint or resentment, this did not go unnoticed by his colleagues and his superior, a man named Chris. One day Chris asked my father, "Clinton, what makes you tick?"

My dad offered a silent prayer and answered, "Jesus Christ."

Chris then began to ask him questions, which led to a lengthy conversation. Eventually, Chris began attending a lunchtime Bible study that took place at work.

God's blessings don't always come in ways we hope for or expect. God may get more glory by our not getting a promotion than by our receiving it. Our job is to seek God first, then leave the results up to him.

On Christian radio, I heard Robbie Symons (pastor of Hope Bible Church in the Toronto area) speaking on these words of Jesus: "Blessed are those who mourn, for they shall be comforted" (Matt. 5:4). I found his message so refreshing after being immersed in a me-centered gospel for many days. Symons was speaking on 2 Corinthians 7:10, where Paul writes that "godly grief produces a repentance that leads to salvation without regret, whereas worldly grief produces death." Symons said:

> Godly sorrow is when I realize that I have hurt God, whereas worldly sorrow is when my life is not going the way I want it to go, and I've been hurt.
>
> Comfort is not a better mattress to sleep on. Comfort is not a new appliance for the kitchen. Comfort is not more financial security. Comfort is not riding in first-class as opposed to economy class. True comfort is knowing the reality that you have been saved from hell. There is no greater comfort—that you've been spared the wrath of God.... True comfort is that you rest in the everlasting arms of the Father. True comfort is that you are a sheep that belongs to the Good Shepherd...
>
> This is the comfort of the gospel message. For those who see their sin, who know its consequences, but then they see their Savior— to believe in Him, to love Him, to be set free from Him, to know the favor of Him, to sing a song of deliverance in Him, to know the supernatural comfort of becoming a child of God—this is the depth and beauty of the gospel.... This is the secret to happiness. This is the secret to blessing.[18]

Giving the gospel without mentioning sin and repentance is like trying to make a lemon meringue pie without lemon or eggs. When you remove key ingredients, the end product isn't the same.

The good news of the gospel begins with the bad news of acknowledging our sin against a holy God. It's not that we've failed to reach our potential; we've failed to reach God's standard, which is perfection.

Edward Luce of *The Financial Times* interviewed Joel Osteen and asked him, "How does telling people to downplay their consciences tally with the New Testament?" Osteen replied, "I preach the gospel, but we are nondenominational. It's not my aim to dwell on technicalities. I want to help people sleep at night."[19]

This is not a minor issue. Sin and repentance are not technicalities; they're at the very heart of the gospel. I share this with you not to be contentious or critical but rather for the sake of truth. "Let God be true though everyone were a liar" (Rom. 3:4).

Paul speaks of the "offense" of the cross (Gal. 5:11). The true gospel offends because it tells people that they're sinners and that their best efforts are not good enough. The gospel is also exclusive—Jesus is the only way to God (John 14:6). In today's society, these are not popular messages. This is why some preachers have come up with a different gospel that appeals to the masses.

Those who choose to follow a me-centered gospel might indeed get their "best life now," because a gospel of self can never lead to eternal life. Jesus said, "For what will it profit a man if he gains the whole world and forfeits his soul? Or what shall a man give in return for his soul?" (Matt. 16:26).

If what Joel Osteen and other self-promoting preachers are teaching is indeed the gospel, then the Bible isn't true.

If, on the other hand, the teachings in the Bible are true, then the self-promoting gospel is false.

REMEMBER

Jesus didn't come to save us from low self-esteem and a bad attitude. He came to save us from the consequence of our sin, which is death.

Ask Yourself

1. What's the problem with sermons that are predominately motivational speeches?

2. Do you think Jesus would feel comfortable in the types of churches mentioned in this chapter? Why or why not?

3. What are the dangers of focusing on prosperity as a goal?

4. How do you respond when you don't get what you think you deserve?

5. What's the danger of a me-centered gospel?

CHAPTER FIFTEEN

The Gospel of Rome

For by grace you have been saved through faith.
And this is not your own doing; it is the gift of God,
not a result of works, so that no one may boast.
Ephesians 2:8-9

Perhaps you know born-again believers in the Catholic Church. So do I.

For many years Doreen attended a Wednesday night prayer meeting and Bible study we held in our home. She faithfully came week after week with her large, well-worn Bible in hand. Each week our meeting began with a time of singing. Inevitably, Doreen would request her favorite gospel song, "Wonderful Words of Life." Although Doreen considered herself Catholic, I never for a moment doubted the reality of her salvation.

The number of Catholics worldwide exceeds 1.3 billion, and they represent almost eighteen percent of the world's population.[1] Since this is such a large group of people, it would be an oversight for me not to address the way of salvation according to the Roman Catholic Church. To accurately represent Catholic beliefs, I'll quote from their own catechism with particular emphasis on the way of salvation.

The original *Catechism of the Council of Trent* was

published in 1566. The *Catechism of the Catholic Church* in use today was commissioned by Pope John Paul II in 1986. A group of twelve cardinals and bishops, chaired by Cardinal Joseph Ratzinger (who would later become Pope Benedict XVI), were entrusted with the task of writing this catechism, which took more than six years.

Roman Catholic Steps to Salvation: Faith

Both Protestants and Catholics agree that faith is necessary for salvation.

"Faith is necessary for salvation,"[2] says the *Catechism of the Catholic Church*, which also states, "Faith is the theological virtue by which we believe in God and believe all that he has said and revealed to us, and that Holy Church proposes for our belief because he is truth itself."[3]

The Bible, meanwhile, teaches that salvation isn't possible without faith (Heb. 11:6). "For by grace you have been saved through faith" (Eph. 2:8).

While on the surface it appears that there's agreement on this between Catholic doctrine and the Bible, Catholics are not referring to faith in Christ alone; they're referring rather to the faith that is "necessary for salvation," which includes an affirmation of the teachings of the Roman Catholic Church.

Roman Catholic Steps to Salvation: Works—The Sacraments

"The Church affirms that for believers, the sacraments of the New Covenant are necessary for salvation."[4] The Catholic Church recognizes seven sacraments: baptism, confirmation, Eucharist, penance, anointing of the sick, holy orders, and matrimony.[5]

The Bible, however, teaches that there's nothing we can do to merit salvation. "For by grace you have been saved through faith. And this is not your own doing; it is the gift of God, not a result of works, so that no one may boast" (Eph. 2:8-9).

Baptism

The Catholic Church teaches that to remove the taint of original sin, a child must be baptized.[6] Baptism is necessary for salvation.[7]

> Holy baptism is the basis of the whole Christian life, the gateway to life in the Spirit, and the door which gives access to the other sacraments. Through baptism we are freed from sin and reborn as sons of God; we become members of Christ; are incorporated into the Church and made sharers in her mission.[8]

If an adult is being baptized in the Catholic Church, they say that it accomplishes the remission of both original and actual sin.[9]

But the Bible teaches that salvation is by faith alone. If water baptism was necessary for salvation, you would expect the Bible to speak of it wherever the gospel is mentioned, yet Paul didn't make it a part of his gospel presentations (1 Cor. 15:1-8). In fact, he says, "For Christ did not send me to baptize but to preach the gospel" (1 Cor. 1:17). If baptism were necessary for salvation, then Paul would have been preaching an incomplete gospel.

The Bible also records incidents of people who were saved without being baptized: the paralytic (Matt. 9:2), the sinful woman (Luke 7:37-50), the tax collector (Luke 18:13-14), and the thief on the cross (Luke 23:39-43).

There are a few passages, however, that seem to indicate that salvation and baptism go together.[10] When reading something in the Bible that appears to contradict other teaching, it's important to remember that the Bible cannot contradict itself. One principle of hermeneutics is that the clear should be used to interpret the unclear.

Confirmation

Roman Catholics believe that confirmation builds on what was begun at baptism:

> The reception of the sacrament of Confirmation is necessary for the completion of baptismal grace.[11]

> It is evident from its celebration that the effect of the sacrament of confirmation is the special outpouring of the Holy Spirit as once granted to the apostles on the day of Pentecost.[12]

Catholics believe that the Holy Spirit comes upon the person being confirmed. Confirmation is considered "a sacrament of initiation, which means that it brings you deeper into communion with the Church."[13]

The Bible teaches that repentant sinners are saved when they acknowledge their need for Jesus as Savior and Lord, and put their faith and trust in Jesus alone (Eph. 2:8-9; Rom. 10:9).

Although confirmation might be viewed as similar to many church membership courses found in Protestant churches today, "it is not the process that causes a person to become a believer, but rather salvation is by grace through faith in Jesus Christ.... No class or confirmation can replace this requirement."[14]

The Bible is silent regarding the ritual of confirmation. A person doesn't come to faith in Christ on a man-made schedule. Salvation can take place anytime and anywhere.

The Eucharist

Catholics are obliged to partake of the Eucharist at least once a year.[15] The catechism explains the Catholic Church's understanding of what takes place during the celebration of the Eucharist:

> It has always been the conviction of the Church of God, and this holy Council now declares again, that by the consecration of the bread and wine there takes place a change of the whole substance of the bread into the substance of the body of Christ our Lord and of the whole substance of the wine into the substance of his blood. This change the holy Catholic Church has fittingly and properly called transubstantiation.[16]

In other words, the Catholic Church teaches that the bread and wine become the actual body and blood of Christ during the Eucharistic prayer of mass. As such, the bread and wine are to be worshiped and adored.[17]

The Eucharist is also known as the Lord's Supper and Communion. All who seek to follow Jesus agree that this is an important part of the Christian faith.

The Bible teaches that we're to partake of the bread and the wine in remembrance of Christ (Luke 22:17-19). "For as often as you eat this bread and drink the cup, you proclaim the Lord's death until he comes" (1 Cor. 11:26).

Nowhere does the Bible teach that we're eating the actual body and drinking the actual blood of Jesus. Theologically, this difference is neither inconsequential nor minor.

As Jesus hung on the cross, he said, "It is finished." This is unlike the sacrifices under the old covenant that had to be repeated. "When Christ had offered for all time a single sacrifice for sins, he sat down at the right hand of God" (Heb.10:12). "For by a single offering he has perfected for all time those who are being sanctified" (Heb. 10:14).

The Bible is clear that Christ's death was a single offering that never needs repeating—unlike the sacrifices of old.

Penance

The sacrament of penance is also known as the sacrament of confession or reconciliation. The *Catholic Encyclopedia*'s lengthy entry for "penance" begins this way:

> Penance is a sacrament of the New Law instituted by Christ in which forgiveness of sins committed after baptism is granted through the priest's absolution to those who with true sorrow confess their sins and promise to satisfy for the same.[18]

The catechism teaches,

> It is through the sacrament of penance that the baptized can be reconciled with God and the Church…. This sacrifice of penance is necessary for salvation for those who have fallen after Baptism. Just as Baptism is necessary for salvation, for those who have not yet been reborn.[19]

Sins must be confessed to a priest who, according to the Roman Catholic Church, has the power to forgive sins. While the Catholic Church affirms that only God can forgive sins,[20] at the same time they say this:

> The disclosure or confession of sins to a priest is an essential element of this sacrament.... It is called the sacrament of forgiveness since by the priest's sacramental absolution God grants the penitent "pardon and peace."[21]

> By Christ's will, the Church possesses the power to forgive the sins of the baptized and exercises it through bishops and priests normally in the sacrament of Penance.[22]

The Bible teaches, "There is one God, and there is one mediator between God and men, the man Christ Jesus" (1 Tim. 2:5). Confession of sin to a priest is nowhere taught in Scripture.

Priests acted as mediators under the old covenant between the people and God, offering sacrifices on their behalf. Once a year on the Day of Atonement (Yom Kippur), the high priest was permitted to enter the Holy of Holies where God's presence dwelled. There was a veil separating the Holy Place from the Holy of Holies (Ex. 26:33). He entered offering blood "for himself and for the unintentional sins of the people" (Heb. 9:7).

The Day of Atonement was a yearly reminder that all of Israel's daily, weekly, and monthly ritual sacrifices and offerings were not enough to atone for sin.

Jesus ushered in the new covenant. John the Baptist announced Jesus' arrival by saying, "Behold the Lamb of God who takes away the sins of the world" (John 1:29).

Jesus died during Passover as the spotless Lamb of God.

Jesus became the perfect and final sacrifice for humanity. At his death, the veil of the temple was torn in two. That veil was thirty feet high, taller than a two-story building. Many speculate on the thickness of the veil, but Scripture doesn't give us that information. The veil was torn from top to bottom, signifying that God has now opened up a way through Jesus to provide us direct access to God; the barrier has been removed.

While preaching the gospel in Athens, Paul said, "The God who made the world and everything in it, being Lord of heaven and earth, does not live in temples made by man" (Acts 17:24). We no longer go to the temple; we *are* the temple (Rom. 12:1).

As Christians, we're a "holy and royal priesthood," as well as a "kingdom of priests" (1 Peter 2:5,9; see also Rev. 1:6; 5:10). This is who we are in Christ, and each and every one of his followers has direct priestly access to the Father through Jesus, who is our High Priest (Heb. 4:14-16).

Anointing of the Sick

This sacrament is sometimes referred to as the viaticum or last rites. It's administered typically to those who are ill, going in for surgery, or dying. The forehead and hands are anointed with oil accompanied by the liturgical prayer asking for the grace of this sacrament.[23]

> The celebration of the sacrament can be preceded by the sacrament of Penance and followed by the sacrament of the Eucharist.[24]

According to the catechism, the special grace of anointing the sick has many effects including "the forgiveness of sins if the sick person was not able to obtain it through the sacrament of Penance" and "the preparation for passing over to eternal life."[25]

The Bible teaches that salvation is not determined by confessing all of one's sins at the moment of death or by being anointed with oil and being prayed over by a priest. Salvation is by faith alone, by grace alone, in Christ alone. Total dependence on Christ without our added works is the only way a person can be saved. A ritual at the time of death can add nothing to our standing before God.

My friend Theresa grew up in a Roman Catholic family. Through the witness of the man who would eventually become her brother-in-law, Theresa professed faith in Christ alone, and so did her mother and several of her siblings. But her father, Robert, showed no interest in the gospel.

After Theresa's mother passed away, her dad met a woman, and they eventually began to live together. One day he began having chest pains, and he was hospitalized. Robert called Theresa's house one night and asked her husband, Jon, to come and see him. When Jon got to the hospital, Theresa's sister was visiting their father. With an urgency in his voice, her dad asked her to leave so he could talk privately to Jon.

He told Jon that he'd called for the priest and had asked for absolution, but the priest had denied his request. The reason given was his common-law living arrangement.

Robert was desperate and asked Jon, "What do you think?"

Jon replied. "It doesn't matter what I think; it only matters what God thinks." Jon then began to walk Robert through the gospel. At a certain point, Robert's eyes seemed to glaze over, and Jon took that as his cue to leave.

When Jon got home, the family prayed together, realizing there was a spiritual battle going on for Robert's soul.

Jon returned to the hospital the next day and once again shared the gospel with Robert. He read 1 Peter 3:18 to him: "Christ also suffered once for sins, the righteous for the unrighteous, that he might bring us to God."

It was beginning to make sense to Robert, and he knew he needed to repent of his sins. He asked Jon, "What do I do?"

Jon replied, "You know how to pray." Robert then dropped his head and asked Christ to save him.

The next day, Jon went again to see Robert and asked him, "What are you going to do when the devil comes accusing you, saying you don't deserve to go to heaven?"

Robert hesitated, then answered, "I guess I'll just send him to Jesus."

Without any coaching on Jon's part, Robert was able to declare that his hope was in Jesus. That was his last coherent conversation; within days, he went to be with his Savior.

The family thanks God that the priest didn't give Robert the false hope of absolution from sin. Robert experienced the true hope of sins forgiven by faith alone, by grace alone, in Christ alone.

Holy Orders

Catholic catechism teaches that Christ entrusted the ministry of reconciliation to bishops and priests who "by virtue of the sacrament of Holy Orders, have the power to forgive all sins in the name of the Father, and of the Son, and of the Holy Spirit."[26]

> Priests must encourage the faithful to come to the sacrament of Penance.[27]

> In converting to Christ through penance and faith, the sinner passes from death to life and does not come into judgment.[28]

The Bible teaches, "Truly, truly, I say to you, whoever hears my word and believes him who sent me has eternal life. He does not come into judgment, but has passed from death to life" (John 5:24).

While conversion involves faith, nowhere does the Bible teach that penance, which involves confession to a priest, is necessary for salvation.

Matrimony

While the Catholic Church teaches that "the sacraments are necessary for salvation," it doesn't mean that each person must receive every sacrament. Matrimony is a perfect example of this. The sacraments provide the opportunity to receive "sacramental grace" that is "proper to each sacrament."[29]

"Sacramental grace is a special help which God gives, to attain the end for which He instituted each Sacrament."[30] The sacrament of matrimony allows spouses to grow in grace.[31]

The Bible teaches that marriage is instituted and blessed by God (Gen. 1:27-28). It is intended to be between one man and one woman for life (1 Cor. 7:2) and faithfulness is required (Heb. 13:4).

Both Catholics and Protestants agree on these teachings about marriage.

We've looked at the doctrines of the Roman Catholic

Church that specifically pertain to salvation. The current catechism as well as the Council of Trent both teach that the church has the mission of teaching and preaching the gospel "so that all men may attain salvation through faith, baptism, and the observance of the commandments."[32] The Catholic formula is thus faith + church + works = salvation.

While many Catholics would disagree and say this isn't true, the proof is in their own documents. I share this not to be divisive but rather out of genuine love and concern for those caught up in a religious system that denies the simple truth of the gospel.

According to the Council of Trent, faith alone is not enough:

> If any one saith, that by faith alone the impious is justified; in such wise as to mean, that nothing else is required to co-operate in order to the obtaining the grace of Justification, and that it is not in any way necessary, that he be prepared and disposed by the movement of his own will; let him be anathema.[33]

The *New St. Joseph Baltimore Catechism* contains a picture of Jesus hanging on the cross with blood flowing from his side. It flows down into a chalice held by a priest. It then overflows out of the chalice through the hands of Mary, until finally it flows to the people of the world. Around this depiction are pictures of each of the other six sacraments. Below the picture is this inscription:

> The sacraments give power to live. They are actions of Christ on our souls. They are

channels or streams flowing from the open side of Christ, through Mary's hands to us.[34]

In 2014, one of the speakers at the Canadian Gideon Convention was Dr. Ben Brown, who at that point had visited China almost 150 times. Many of those visits were by invitation of the China Christian Council, which was formed following the Cultural Revolution. The China Christian Council is an umbrella organization for all Protestant churches in the People's Republic of China and is overseen by the Communist Party of China.

Dr. Brown explained that there are five government-sanctioned religions in China: Buddhism, Taoism, Islam, Christianity (Protestantism), and Catholicism. Dr. Brown said,

> Catholics weren't considered inside of Christianity as far as the government of China was concerned, then or now. They had their own group. They were allowed to be there; it was legal; it still is. When the Catholics protested and said, "No we're Christians," the government said, "No, you're not, you're sacerdotal."

Sacerdotalism is defined as "religious belief emphasizing the powers of priests as essential mediators between God and humankind."[35] This theological term indicates that Catholics are not grace-based but church-based; salvation is through the church, not the gospel. This distinction was observed by the communist government of China. They saw what even many Christians fail to see: The teachings of the Catholic Church and the Bible are incompatible.

I opened this chapter telling you about a Catholic lady

named Doreen, who I felt sure had a personal relationship with Jesus. It's important to realize that any born-again Christians within the Roman Catholic Church are Christians despite the church, not because of it.

It's impossible to be saved by following the man-made formula—faith plus the church plus works—that's taught by the Roman Catholic Church.

Salvation is available to all who in simple faith place their trust in the finished work of Christ on the cross alone. They pass from death to life, and nothing and no one can snatch them out of the Father's hand (John 5:24; 10:27-28).

> When the kindness of God our Savior and His love for mankind appeared, he saved us, not on the basis of deeds which we have done in righteousness, but according to his mercy, by the washing of regeneration and renewing by the Holy Spirit (Titus 3:4-5).

REMEMBER

The way a person lives give evidence of true faith but does nothing toward gaining salvation.

Ask Yourself

1. According to Roman Catholicism, what must a person do to be saved?

2. According to the Bible, what must a person do to be saved?

3. What does this verse mean? "For there is one God and one mediator between God and mankind, the man Christ Jesus" (1 Tim. 2:5).

4. The apostle Paul said, "I do not treat the grace of God as meaningless. For if keeping the law could make us right with God, then there was no need for Christ to die" (Gal. 2:21). How does this verse relate to the Catholic Church's teaching on the necessity of the sacraments for salvation?

5. If the Bible teaches salvation is by faith alone, by grace alone, and in Christ alone, what does this say about the role of the sacraments?

CHAPTER SIXTEEN

Light versus Darkness

If we claim to have fellowship with him
and yet walk in the darkness,
we lie and do not live out the truth.
1 John 1:6

Have you ever known anyone who suffered from optophobia? Optophobia is the fear of opening one's eyes.

Believe it or not, this is a real fear that some people have. A person with this phobia prefers to remain in the darkness rather than open their eyes and see the light of day. Likely there are psychological reasons for this, but by way of analogy, imagine choosing darkness over light.

Futurist Jolene Creighton wrote,

> Most of us already know that darkness is the
> absence of light, and that light travels at the
> fastest speed possible for a physical object. So,
> what does this mean? In short, it means that
> the moment that light leaves, darkness returns.[1]

In other words, if I'm not walking in the light, I'm walking in darkness. What does it mean to walk in darkness? Ephesians 5:3-5, 11-12 (NIV) answers that question by giving us a list of activities practiced by those who are walking in darkness:

> But among you there must not be even a hint of sexual immorality, or of any kind of impurity, or of greed, because these are improper for God's holy people. Nor should there be obscenity, foolish talk, or coarse joking, which are out of place, but rather thanksgiving. For of this, you can be sure: No immoral, impure, or greedy person—such a person is an idolater—has any inheritance in the kingdom of Christ and of God.... Have nothing to do with the fruitless deeds of darkness, but rather expose them. It is shameful even to mention what the disobedient do in secret.

Similar lists are given in three other passages that speak to the heart of our holy God, reflecting his complete disdain for ungodly behavior. These lists don't just contain suggestions of things you might want to avoid; rather, God is saying, "If these activities are characteristic of your life, then you're not saved." On my own, I wouldn't have the nerve to speak so boldly, but this is the Word of God, and this is his standard.

Here are those three other passages. Look at them closely:

> The acts of the flesh are obvious: sexual immorality, impurity, and debauchery; idolatry and witchcraft; hatred, discord, jealousy, fits of rage, selfish ambition, dissensions, factions, and envy; drunkenness, orgies, and the like. I warn you, as I did before, that those who live like this will not inherit the kingdom of God" (Gal. 5:19-21 NIV).

> Don't you realize that those who do wrong will

not inherit the Kingdom of God? Don't fool yourselves. Those who indulge in sexual sin, or who worship idols, or commit adultery, or are male prostitutes, or practice homosexuality, or are thieves, or greedy people, or drunkards, or are abusive, or cheat people—none of these will inherit the Kingdom of God. Some of you were once like that. But you were cleansed; you were made holy; you were made right with God by calling on the name of the Lord Jesus Christ and by the Spirit of our God" (1 Cor. 6:9-11 NLT).

The night is far gone; the day is at hand. So then let us cast off the works of darkness and put on the armor of light. Let us walk properly as in the daytime, not in orgies and drunkenness, not in sexual immorality and sensuality, not in quarreling and jealousy. But put on the Lord Jesus Christ, and make no provision for the flesh, to gratify its desires (Rom. 13:12-14).

Darkness and light cannot coexist. If you're a child of God, these listed activities will not characterize your life. That's not to say that a true believer will never fall. We're all sometimes guilty of doing things we wished we hadn't done. The difference, though, is that when a true believer sins, he'll come under conviction. If one of these activities is present in your life and there's no conviction, that's a good indicator that there's no true faith—and therefore, no salvation. While sin is a reality in all our lives, ongoing, habitual sin should concern those who call themself Christian.

I'm quite aware that what I'm writing here is not

politically correct, and there are many who would take offense with these words.

To put things in perspective, we must remember that those who repent of their sins and put their faith and trust in the Lord Jesus Christ have been made right with God and are forgiven. Their sins will never be held against them. This is the promise for all who are genuinely born again:

> Some of you were once like that. But you were cleansed; you were made holy; you were made right with God by calling on the name of the Lord Jesus Christ and by the Spirit of our God (1 Cor. 6:11 NLT).

Here are questions we need to ask ourselves: Am I walking in the light, or am I walking in darkness? What characterizes my life? Are the deeds of darkness a part of my life? Do I desire holiness, and am I striving for it?

God's Word tells us, "Be holy; without holiness, no one will see the Lord" (Heb. 12:14 NIV).

As we've seen, the Bible clearly describes deeds of darkness and states that people who make a practice of these activities will not inherit the kingdom of God. How is it possible that with so many passages on this subject, a large number of professing Christians disregard what's being said and continue to walk in darkness? How can you or I excuse these behaviors and claim to be right with God?

Each of us will stand before a holy God one day and give account (see Matt. 12:36; Rom. 14:12).

God is gracious, loving, and merciful. He longs to forgive us and has provided a way for all our sins to be forgiven. He says, "These are the ones I look on with favor: those who are humble and contrite in spirit, and who tremble at my word" (Isa. 66:2 NIV).

God is holy and calls us to be holy. If you choose to live a lifestyle contrary to him, then according to Scripture it's clear that you don't know him. The Bible says, "Don't fool yourselves" (1 Cor. 6:9 NLT), and "Do not be deceived" (Gal. 6:7).

Jesus tells us, "I am the light of the world. Whoever follows me shall not walk in darkness, but will have the light of life" (John 8:12).

Jesus also said,

> I have come into the world as light so that whoever believes in me may not remain in darkness. If anyone hears my words and does not keep them, I do not judge him; for I did not come to judge the world but to save the world. The one who rejects me and does not receive my words has a judge; the word that I have spoken will judge him on the last day (John 12:46-48).

> And this is the judgment: the light has come into the world, and people loved the darkness rather than the light because their works were evil (John 3:19).

REMEMBER

If I'm not walking in the light, I'm walking in darkness.

Ask Yourself

1. What are the "deeds of darkness" listed in Ephesians 5:3-5, Galatians 5:19-21, 1 Corinthians 6:9-10, and Romans 13:12-14

2. What is the warning given to those who persist in "deeds of darkness?"

3. How can we tell if we're walking in the light?

4. When you sin, do you sense the conviction of the Holy Spirit over what you've done? Describe.

5. What's the difference between committing a sin and having sin as the pattern of your life?

CHAPTER SEVENTEEN

The Mystery of Salvation

If you confess with your mouth that Jesus is Lord
and believe in your heart that God raised him from
the dead, you will be saved.

Romans 10:9

Salvation is a supernatural event; no cajoling in the world can bring about spiritual life. Here's a true story of men trying to do the work only God can do.

Bert and his wife received an invitation to attend the play *Heaven's Gates and Hell's Flames* at a local church. The play consists of a series of vignettes depicting people who, based on their choices, find themselves in either heaven or hell. Following the play, the local pastor gave a short gospel message followed by an altar call inviting people to come to the front of the church and give their hearts to Jesus.

Despite the pastor's impassioned plea, no one went forward, so he began to preach some more, followed by another call to the altar. After three or four people went forward, the preacher appeared frustrated by the poor response and shouted out, "That's not enough!"

He then made a third altar call, adding that he felt some were there who wanted to come forward but needed encouragement. He told the congregation that "encouragers" at the back of the church would be guided by the Holy Spirit to individuals there who wanted to be saved but needed encouragement.

The person who played Jesus in the play came beside Bert and said to him, "The Holy Spirit told me you want to go up to the front and be saved." He then offered to go up to the front with him.

Surprised by this, Bert told the young man, "I've been saved for five years, so that can't be the voice of the Holy Spirit you heard." The Jesus actor seemed embarrassed and didn't know what to say or do.

That experience confirmed to Bert that this type of altar call is not scriptural and can lead people into an emotional experience and often a false profession. Although the play was well done and could have been used by God to bring conviction of sin, the problem arose with the preacher's promptings and pressure. Salvation is a work of God. We're responsible only to preach a clear and faithful gospel message, and then pray and leave the results to God (1 Cor. 3:6).

———

In John 1:12-13, we read this about Jesus: "But to all who did receive him, who believed in his name, he gave the right to become children of God, who were born, not of blood nor of the will of the flesh nor of the will of man, but of God." These words make clear that no one is saved by sheer human will.

William MacDonald, in his commentary on the gospel of John, makes this observation:

> Salvation is not passed down from parent to child through the blood stream. A person does

not have the power in his own flesh or will to produce the new birth. The power to produce the new birth does not rest with anything or anyone but God.[1]

My parents' faith can't save me. No human being can save another human being. No preacher, parent, or friend has the power to produce the new birth. As Bible teacher A. W. Pink said,

> The whole work of the Spirit within the elect is to plant in the heart a hatred for and a loathing of *sin as sin,* and a love for and a longing after *holiness as holiness.* This is something which no human power can bring about. It is something which the most faithful preaching as such cannot produce. It is something which the mere circulating and reading of Scripture does not impart. It is a miracle of *grace,* a divine wonder which none but God can or does perform.[2]

The Man Who Was Saved by His Own Sermon

As a young man, William Haslam became very ill and was told by three doctors that he would not recover. God spared his life, however, and when Haslam regained his health and strength, he determined to live to the glory of God. He thought that his acceptance by God depended on his works, which made him diligent in prayer, fasting, and giving.

Haslam's dedication to God led to his ordination by the Church of England in 1842. At the ordination service, the bishop addressed the new ministers, stressing that they were going to be responsible for the souls of their parishioners.

This didn't sit well with Haslam, because he wanted to be a clergyman who read prayers, preached sermons, and tried to get people to come out to church. Answering for souls who would live forever was not what he had in mind. In his own soul, he lacked peace and assurance.

Haslam preached on holy living, not conversion. As different people in his parish told him stories of their conversion, he wondered what this "conversion" could be.

One day Haslam was reading a tract and came to these words: "Then shall He say unto them, Depart from Me; I never knew you." These words shook him as he thought, *What if God says that to me?* Then he thought, *I've given up the world; I love God; I visit the sick; I have daily service and weekly communion. But what if God says he doesn't know me?* These thoughts overwhelmed him.

The Holy Spirit began to convict Haslam as he considered the dreadful thought: *What if I'm wrong!* Added to this, he couldn't bear the thought of all those he had misled.

For several days Haslam was in a state of desperation as he considered these matters.

When Sunday morning came, he felt so ill that he didn't think he would be able to preach. But before he could decide to cancel the service, he heard the church bells ringing and decided to go and give a few readings, before dismissing the people.

He walked up to the pulpit and read the text for the day, Matthew 22:42: "What think ye of Christ?"

As he began to explain the passage, he realized that the Pharisees and scribes didn't know that Jesus was the Son of God or that he'd come to save them. As Haslam spoke, he began to realize that he himself was no better than the Pharisees.

There and then he began to see what the Pharisees didn't see, and his soul was filled with the joy of the Lord.

A visiting preacher was in the congregation that day. Suddenly he stood, put up his arms, and shouted, "The parson is converted! The parson is converted! Hallelujah!" Immediately his shouts were drowned out by the shouts and praises of three or four hundred of the congregation.

The news spread everywhere that the parson had been converted by his own sermon in his own pulpit. At the evening service, the church couldn't hold the crowds that came. During that service Haslam said, "If I had died last week, I should have been lost forever."

After years of serving God without truly knowing him, William Haslam was born again. He trusted Christ and experienced the grace of God in his life. From that day onward, he was committed to preaching nothing but the truth of God's Word. In 1880 he wrote *From Death into Life* recounting his spiritual journey. He said, "This is not, as biographies generally are, an account of life on to death, but rather the other way—a narrative of transition from death into life."[3]

God Sees Our Hearts

While conviction of the Holy Spirit and repentance are necessary in all true conversions, people get to that place in different ways.

Recently my longtime friend Graham informed me that his father was very ill and not expected to live much longer. He was concerned for his father's salvation and asked for prayer.

I began to pray for Mr. Hardie, and also decided I wanted to visit him, hoping for one last chance to share the gospel. Mr. Hardie grew up attending church and was a member of the Boys Brigade in Scotland. He'd heard the gospel many times before.

I walked into his hospital room, Bible in hand, but what happened next wasn't at all what I'd anticipated. As I began talking about the Lord, Mr. Hardie beamed back at me and said, "I love him just as he loves me. He's my Savior."

"Good news to hear," I said.

He smiled and replied, "Very good news to me."

I started making notes of the things he was saying, knowing I would never remember it all.

Speaking of the past, he said, "I thought I could look after myself, but I was wrong. It took a long time, but now I know—no doubting Thomas…. No one will separate me from Jesus, no one. I love him so much."

Spoken as a prayer to the Lord, he said, "I love you so much. I wish I'd come sooner. But better late than never."

He expressed concern for his family, saying, "I wish they were all Christians."

I read from Psalm 139. He asked for Psalm 23. I also read Matthew 20 about the workers and how they all got the same wage regardless of when they came. I shared that Jesus accepts us no matter how late we come to him. I read a few other psalms, as well as Romans 8 about how nothing can separate us from the love of God.

At the end of our conversation, Mr. Hardie spoke of the peace he felt.

As I left the hospital room, I felt confused. I was thrilled to see Mr. Hardie's obvious love for the Lord and felt no doubt in my mind that he was saved. But before I walked into that room, neither I nor his son Graham had thought that Mr. Hardie was a Christian. When did this change in his life occur?

When I got home, I immediately wrote to Graham to tell him what had happened. Here's an excerpt from his letter back to me:

> It is through tears that I read of your report.... Sometimes the Spirit raises the dead early; other times it's a slow process. Even though his heart was hard, it softened as time went on.... I have no doubt now and look forward to being reunited with Mum and Dad.

Graham went to see his dad not long after my visit, and less than forty-eight hours later, his father had passed from this life to the next. Here's an excerpt from Graham's account:

> My Dad breathed his last breath today.... I saw him after your visit and his love for Jesus was clearly evident. It was like a weight was lifted off his body. I've never seen him filled with such joy. It was like witnessing a man raised from the dead.

As I tried to make sense of what occurred in Mr. Hardie's life, I finally concluded that I had witnessed Romans 10:9 in action: "If you confess with your mouth that Jesus is Lord and believe in your heart that God raised him from the dead, you will be saved."

Mr. Hardie prayed no sinner's prayer. I believe that during that short time we spent together in the hospital room, Mr. Hardie finally stopped fighting against God and chose to embrace him. As he confessed with his mouth and believed in his heart, he was saved.

No outward prayer was necessary. God sees our hearts.

While conviction of the Holy Spirit is necessary to draw a person to salvation, we must not neglect our part, which is sharing the gospel.

Many years ago, I attended a presentation by Rico Tyce, founder of the evangelistic outreach program Christianity Explored. He told of his grandmother's final week of life. He said she was trusting in her goodness to gain acceptance by God rather than placing her faith in Jesus Christ. Although he knew her spiritual condition, he didn't speak with her about Jesus. Afraid of what she or his family would think, he remained silent. With deep regret he told us that in that moment, he loved himself more than he loved her.

Like Rico Tyce, I've sometimes held back from sharing the gospel out of fear over what people will think. We need to remind ourselves that we're never responsible for the outcome, but we are responsible to tell others.

REMEMBER

While conviction of the Holy Spirit and repentance are necessary in all true conversions, people get to that place in different ways.

Ask Yourself

1. What do you think is the danger of pressuring someone to make an immediate decision for Christ?

2. If you have a salvation experience, did it come quickly, or was it a longer process?

3. What good works did Mr. Haslam count on to ensure his right standing with God before he was converted?

4. What was the evidence of conversion in Mr. Hardie's life?

5. What do you think "Depart from me" will entail?

CHAPTER EIGHTEEN

The Wrath of God

*He will pour out his anger and wrath on those who
live for themselves, who refuse to obey the truth and
instead live lives of wickedness.*
Romans 2:8 NLT

"In Christ Alone" was the first hymn that Keith Getty and Stuart Townend wrote together, and it's their most popular. A controversy arose in 2013 when the US Presbyterian Committee on Congregational Song chose to exclude the song "In Christ Alone" from its new hymnal *Glory to God* because of objectionable content found in the second stanza.

> In Christ alone, Who took on flesh,
>   fullness of God in helpless babe!
> This gift of love and righteousness,
>   scorned by the ones He came to save.
> Till on that cross as Jesus died,
>   the wrath of God was satisfied;
> For ev'ry sin on Him was laid—
>   here in the death of Christ, I live.[1]

The Gettys were approached by the Presbyterian committee with the request to alter the lyrics from "as Jesus died | the wrath of God was satisfied" to "Till on that cross as Jesus died | the love of God was magnified."

The songwriters wouldn't allow the changes because "it was considered too great a departure from their original words."[2] The committee then had to decide whether to include the song with the original lyrics or to remove it from the hymnal altogether. They put it to a vote, which led to six in favor of inclusion and nine against. This failed to reach the two-thirds majority necessary for a song to be included in the hymnal.

Different people weighed in on this issue via articles and talk shows, with the focus being on the word *wrath*. In a formal statement addressing the issue, Mary Louise Bringle, the hymnal committee chair, denied that the word *wrath* was the reason that line was altered and claimed that the issue was actually the word *satisfied*.[3]

Regardless of the reason for removing the word *wrath* from the hymnal, the fact remains that God's wrath is not a popular subject.

What Is Wrath?

According to the Oxford Dictionary, wrath is another way of saying "extreme anger." Can you remember the last time you heard a sermon on the wrath of God? How about the love of God? There's no shortage of messages on the love of God.

This is not a new problem. In the second century, a heresy was promulgated by Marcion of Sinope. He believed the God of the Old Testament was not the same as the God of the New Testament. He, too, had a problem with the wrath of God. What King Solomon said almost three thousand years ago holds true: "There is nothing new under the sun" (Eccl. 1:9).

Tertullian, a contemporary of Marcion, wrote a book called *Against Marcion* in which he makes this statement:

> A better god has been discovered, one who is neither offended nor angry nor inflicts punishment, who has prepared no fire in hell, no gnashing of teeth in the outer darkness! He is purely and simply good. He indeed forbids all delinquency, but only in word…
>
> Afraid to condemn what he really condemns, afraid to hate what he does not love, permitting that to be done which he does not allow…. What new god is there, except a false one?[4]

Can the wrath of God and the love of God coexist? I believe not only that they can coexist but that they *must* coexist. God is not one-dimensional, and neither are we—which makes sense, because we're made in the image of God.

I need to clarify that the anger of God is not the same as the anger of man. God's anger is holy, just, and fair. According to J. I. Packer, "God's wrath in the Bible is never the capricious, self-indulgent, irritable, morally ignoble thing that human anger so often is. It is, instead, a right and necessary reaction to objective moral evil."[5]

If God is angry, it's natural to ask why. By looking at some passages in both the Old and New Testaments, we'll see some things that make God angry.

• Lack of obedience

> Great is the wrath of the LORD that is kindled against us, because our fathers have not obeyed the words of this book, to do according to all that is written concerning us (2 Kings 22:13).

God's wrath comes on those who are disobedient (Eph. 5:6 NIV).

(*Additional passages*: Col. 3:6; Rom. 2:8; 2 Chron. 34:21; John 3:36; Jer. 7:29)

- **Idolatry**

   Why do you provoke me to anger with the works of your hands, making offerings to other gods in the land of Egypt where you have come to live, so that you may be cut off and become a curse and a taunt among all the nations of the earth? (Jer. 44:8).

   Put to death therefore what is earthly in you: sexual immorality, impurity, passion, evil desire, and covetousness, which is idolatry. On account of these the wrath of God is coming (Col. 3:5-6).

   (*Additional passages*: Jer. 7:18-20; 2 Kings 22:17; Eph. 5:5)

- **Stealing**

   Didn't divine anger fall on the entire community of Israel when Achan, a member of the clan of Zerah, sinned by stealing the things set apart for the LORD? He was not the only one who died because of his sin (Josh. 22:20 NLT).

- **Pride**

   And when he humbled himself the wrath of the Lord turned from him, so as not to make a complete destruction (2 Chron. 12:12).

   (*Additional passage*: 2 Chron. 32:26)

- **Refusing to Acknowledge and Call on the Lord**

  > Pour out your wrath on the nations that refuse to acknowledge you—and on the peoples that do not call upon your name (Jer. 10:25 NLT).

- **Ungodliness**

  > The wrath of God is being revealed from heaven against all the godlessness and wickedness of people, who suppress the truth by their wickedness (Rom. 1:18 NIV).

This is not an exhaustive list, but it's comprehensive enough to show that God hates sin.

Many believe that a loving God would never condemn anyone to hell. They feel that because of his love, he should be all-forgiving. If God just forgave everyone, then heaven would look an awful lot like earth—full of murder, immorality, lying, greed, and selfishness.

A mother who allows her child to do whatever he or she wants is deemed a bad parent. Consequences of actions are understood in family relations as well as in society. If a mass murderer stood before a judge, and the judge allowed him to go free without paying for his crime, society would be in an uproar demanding justice.

We're like that mass murderer. Jesus said,

> You have heard that it was said to those of old, "You shall not murder; and whoever murders will be liable to judgment." But I say to you that everyone who is angry with his brother will be liable to judgment; whoever insults his brother will be liable to the council; and whoever says, "You fool!" will be liable to the hell of fire (Matt. 5:21, 22).

God's standard is much higher than man's, and by God's standard we're all guilty. It's interesting how many hold a double standard when it comes to God. The law of cause and effect is valid in human relationships, but somehow God's love is distorted into the kind of love that always says yes, never corrects, and allows unspeakable evil without so much as a slap on the hand.

God's wrath is in proportion to his hatred for sin. We have a high tolerance for sin, whereas God has zero tolerance for sin. Despite his hatred for sin, God has no desire to punish anyone. He says, "I have no pleasure in the death of the wicked, but that the wicked turn from his way and live" (Ezek. 33:11). God's wrath is balanced by his incredible love: "The Lord is merciful and gracious, slow to anger and abounding in steadfast love" (Ps. 103:8).

We see this modeled in God's dealings with wicked, idolatrous Israel:

> Return, faithless Israel, declares the Lord. I will not look on you in anger, for I am merciful, declares the Lord; I will not be angry forever. Only acknowledge your guilt, that you rebelled against the Lord your God and scattered your favors among foreigners under every green tree, and that you have not obeyed my voice, declares the Lord. Return, O faithless children, declares the Lord; for I am your master (Jer. 3:12-14).

A day of wrath has been predicted as far back as the book of Job, which is the oldest book in the Bible, and which tells us, "The wicked are reserved for the day of doom; they shall be brought out on the day of wrath" (Job 21:30 NKJV).

The reality of a future day of judgment was clearly understood by those living in Bible times.

The prophet Joel predicts the doom of the wrath of God, then writes these beautiful words of love and compassion immediately following:

The day of the Lord is an awesome, terrible thing.
Who can possibly survive?
That is why the Lord says,
"Turn to me now, while there is time.
Give me your hearts.
Come with fasting, weeping, and mourning.
Don't tear your clothing in your grief,
but tear your hearts instead."
Return to the Lord your God,
for he is merciful and compassionate,
slow to get angry and filled with unfailing love.
He is eager to relent and not punish
(Joel 2:11-13 NLT).

That is who our God is. His character demands justice—he cannot turn a blind eye to sin. Yet his love and compassion are continually extended toward us, bidding us come to find forgiveness.

John MacArthur makes an interesting observation about how God has expressed his wrath from the beginning of time to his final show of wrath at the end of time:

Throughout all of that period, the strangest paradox is working. And that very strange paradox is this, that all the way through the expression of God's wrath up until His ultimate final and eternal wrath, God is busily working to save sinners from His own wrath.

> Therein lies the marvelous reality of the nature of God that encompasses both righteousness and holiness alongside mercy and grace that makes justice and judgment the twin of love and kindness.[6]

Justice says, "The wages of sin is death" (Rom. 6:23). Love says, "He himself bore our sins in his body on the tree" (1 Peter 2:24).

It's at the cross that God's love and justice meet. Sin is so offensive to God that it has to be punished. Out of God's great love, that punishment fell on Jesus, the perfect, sinless Lamb of God. "Without the shedding of blood, there is no forgiveness of sins" (Heb. 9:22).

One of the most beautiful passages in all of Scripture is Isaiah 53. Written prophetically about seven hundred years before Christ, it graphically depicts the suffering of the Lord.

This is the passage of Scripture that was instrumental in my mother coming to the Lord at age thirteen. Although she attended church regularly, she knew she wasn't saved. One day a friend invited her to a gospel meeting, and she gladly accepted the invitation. After the meeting, a man began to share different Scriptures with my mother, as she'd expressed interest in salvation. She knew all the Bible verses he was quoting her, and nothing was getting through.

Finally, he asked her to read Isaiah 53:5 and to replace the pronoun meaning everybody with her own name. For example, in her case, "He was pierced for Joyce's rebellion." In reading it through like that, the message of the gospel finally pierced her heart, and she gave her life to the Lord.

Here's a paraphrase of Isaiah 53:3-6 with personal replacements in italics:

He was despised and rejected—
a man of sorrows, acquainted with deepest grief.
I turned *my* back on him and looked the other way.
He was despised, and *I* did not care.
Yet it was *my* weaknesses he carried;
it was *my* sorrows that weighed him down.
And we thought his troubles were a punishment from God,
a punishment for his own sins!
But he was pierced for *my* rebellion,
crushed for *my* sins.
He was beaten so *I* could be whole.
He was whipped so *I* could be healed.
Like a sheep, *I* have strayed away.
I have left God's paths to follow *my* own.
Yet the Lord laid *my sins* on him (Isa. 53:3-6 NLT).

The love of God and the wrath of God are in perfect balance. When we grasp that truth, we're able to see God more clearly.

REMEMBER

God must be true to his character, which demands justice; he cannot turn a blind eye to sin. Yet his love and compassion are continually extended toward us, bidding us come to find forgiveness.

Ask Yourself

1. What are some sins God hates?

2. Is my life characterized by behaviors that will incur the wrath of God?

3. What would be the result of God not punishing anyone?

4. How do justice and love meet in God's character?

5. How can we be sure of avoiding God's wrath at the end of time?

CHAPTER NINETEEN

The Great Reveal

The Lord knows those who are his…
Let everyone who names the name of the Lord
depart from iniquity.
2 Timothy 2:19

When I was growing up, there was a game show on TV called *To Tell the Truth*. Three contestants would make identical "My name is—" statements, each claiming to be a certain person whose brief (and interesting) bio was then read aloud to a panel of celebrities. The celebrity panelists would then ask questions of the contestants in order to correctly guess the right person. While answering the questions, the two imposters were allowed to lie, while the real person had to tell the truth.

To end the game, a vote was taken, followed by the catchphrase, "Would the real [person's name] please stand up?" For a few seconds, each contestant would pretend to stand, until finally the real person stood to reveal his or her identity. This would often come as a surprise, since the answers given to questions were quite believable.

Someday there will be a great reveal in heaven when God identifies those who are truly his. "God's firm foundation stands, bearing this seal: 'The Lord knows those who are his,' and, "Let everyone who names the name of the Lord depart from iniquity'" (2 Tim. 2:19).

God is a loving father, but he is also a righteous and holy judge.

———•◦•———

I'm now going to tell you about four people and give you an opportunity to play a variation of the game seen on *To Tell the Truth*. I'll list some facts about each person's life up to a certain point. Your job is to decide which ones you think are truly saved. Then I'll tell you the rest of each person's story.

Dave Gass

- A devout follower of Jesus for forty years
- Fully devoted to studying the Scriptures
- Memorized eighteen books of the Bible
- Read through the entire Bible twenty-three times
- Evangelical pastor for twenty years

Charo Washer

- Asked Jesus into her heart at age fourteen while attending a Christian school
- Active in church
- Felt God was calling her to be a missionary at age sixteen
- Married a missionary at age twenty
- Together with her husband, served for twelve years in Peru

Gary Shriver

- Prayed a prayer of salvation while in his late twenties
- Married with three children

- Attended an evangelical church
- Was involved in music ministry
- Had an adulterous affair for three years

Megan Hill

- Raised by godly Christian parents
- Doesn't remember a time when she didn't love Jesus
- By age three or four, had embraced God as Creator, Jesus as her Savior, the Spirit as her Helper, and the Bible as her guide.
- Attended Christian school
- Has no memory of becoming a Christian

It would be presumptuous of me to tell you which of these individuals are truly saved. But I can tell you what they've said and how they declare themselves today.

Dave Gass: The Rest of the Story

On April 30, 2019, Dave Gass tweeted, "I'm not a Christian anymore…. I am walking away from faith. Even though this has been a massive bomb drop in my life, it has been decades in the making."

He went on to say,

> As an adult my marriage was a sham and a constant source of pain for me. I did everything I was supposed to—marriage workshops, counseling, Bible reading together, date nights every week, marriage books—but my marriage never became what I was promised it would be…. I traveled on speaking teams, preached to thousands of teenagers at a time, wrote blogs, was published, formed curriculum, taught

workshops, was an up-and-comer reforming my denomination. The whole time hoping at some point it would click, and become true for me.[1]

Justin Thuttle was a deacon at Grace Family Fellowship where Dave Gass pastored. He posted on Twitter that Gass wasn't entirely forthcoming about his faith journey, and he branded Gass as an unrepentant sinner. Shortly after that revelation, Thuttle posted the following on social media:

> Yes, he was my pastor when he "walked away." He actually just slept with a married woman in the church and got caught. He never repented, and they still live together. Last year all the information came to light. The affair happened for almost a year before it was uncovered. So the whole "I did everything right in my marriage" part was kinda funny, until I saw how many people liked his story.[2]

Another social media user summarized the situation this way:

> Sadly this is the story of someone who never knew the gospel, Jesus, or the Holy Spirit. Bible knowledge, left alone, cannot and will not save you. Frankly, you can't walk away from a genuine faith you never had to begin with. There's still hope for this guy.[3]

The apostle John says this about the "many antichrists" who eventually turn away from God's true people: "They went out from us, but they were not of us; for if they had been of us, they would have continued with us. But they went out, that it might become plain that they all are not of us" (1 John 2:19).

Charo Washer: The Rest of the Story

At the age of thirty-two, Charo Washer realized that she was not saved. This came as quite a shock to those who knew her. Some well-meaning friends had a hard time believing that Charo wasn't saved earlier. They said, "It's not that you were not saved, it's just that we kind of grow cold in our love for God at times. Look at you, you've been a missionary for twelve years."

Charo knew her own heart; she knew that she'd been empty for years.

Although she'd responded to an invitation and prayed a sinner's prayer, she realized she hadn't repented and acknowledged her sin. She had merely been asked if she wanted Jesus, and she thought, *Why not?*

Charo was a good kid who hung around with Christian kids. It was easy to dress like a Christian, look like a Christian, and go to church as her friends did. She didn't go drinking since her friends didn't drink. It was easy to fit into their mold.

Charo was active in church but never really had a desire to read the Bible. She would read haphazardly out of duty, but she had no love for God's Word. She would pray for people to be saved, but it was just a to-do list.

Even though Charo came to realize that she was unsaved during the time she was serving the Lord in Peru, God still used her to share the gospel. She had a love for missions and for people, and she wanted to evangelize. Her explanation for this is that God can speak through a mule.

She struggled to appear godly. When preaching was going on, her mind would be on the grocery list or other things. Charo realized there was no power in her life to overcome sin, and no zeal. She would beat herself up all the time, saying, "I just have to buckle down and do this," or "I need to stop doing this." She would wonder why it was so hard to forgive. She was critical in her heart. She knew that those who belong to the Lord should have peace, but she had no peace.

After returning to the United States from Peru, her husband Paul visited several churches where he gave a message titled "How Do You Know if You're a Christian?" Charo would squirm in her seat, She thought, *How do I just go through this test and feel okay at the end?*

She struggled for about three years before admitting to herself that she wasn't a Christian. Her heart had not been changed. She realized that she was putting something off that could mean eternity without Christ.

One day she was sitting outside and saw a prostitute going up and down the street. *I'm no better than she is*, she thought. *You can see her sin. It's so easy to look pretty and wear a long skirt, and nobody knows.*

God opened her eyes at that point. One day, her husband said to her during a car ride, "All I delight in is just being in God's will." She knew she didn't delight in that, and finally told her husband everything.

"From what you told me," he said, "I can't tell you that you're a Christian."

When they got home, she read through the book of 1 John and went through the evidence for faith written there. Before that point, she'd never really realized that she was a sinner. That evening it became very personal as God showed her who she really was. She cried out to God in confession and repentance, and God saved her.[4]

Gary Shriver: The Rest of the Story

In the midst of his adultery, Gary felt God chasing him and wooing him back. Gary cried out repeatedly to God, "Help me! Help me!" God did help him, using books, sermons, and conversations to show him his need to confess and repent. The conviction that the affair was a sinful relationship became stronger.

Despite the conviction Gary felt, he repeated for three years the cycle of adultery, confession, and vowing to never do it again. The situation came to a head when Gary was confronted by an employee at his company about the affair. The employee quoted Matthew 18:15-17 to him and said, "If you don't come clean, I'll tell our pastor about the affair."

This was the impetus Gary needed to break this cycle of sin. Finally, after three years of wrestling with God, Gary was broken and realized he couldn't go on like that. With tears streaming down his face, he confessed his sin to his pastor.

Gary went home immediately to confess to his wife of nineteen years. Mona knew something was wrong by the look on Gary's face. Then he said, "I've been unfaithful to you."

As Gary confessed, repented, and took ownership of his actions, he was once again able to sense the presence of the Lord in his life. Gary says, "I had slipped into sin subtly and slowly, and no one had known. It was surprising how easily it happened, how easily I could live a double life. At the time, I thought I was close to God, but I had fallen into Satan's snare just as easily as some dumb animal gets trapped by following its instincts."

Gary's relationship with the Lord is strong today, as is his relationship with his wife. Together with another couple, Gary and Mona started a ministry called Hope and Healing. Its purpose is to offer support, encouragement, and hope to couples who've experienced the heartache of adultery.[5]

Megan Hill: The Rest of the Story

Megan has what many would consider a boring Christian testimony. She loved Jesus as a child, and she still does. She doesn't remember praying a prayer of salvation, or ever walking the aisle to the altar. She never had a eureka moment.

In the fifth grade, Megan began attending a Christian school where chapel services often included dramatic testimonies from ex-drug addicts, former atheists, and others. She never heard stories of ordinary people like herself, which led her to fear she hadn't really been saved—or at least that her story of being saved wasn't quite legitimate.

Megan began to question whether she'd been saved at all. She became convinced that her testimony was inferior. While just a teenager Megan had tears in her eyes when she sang the words of Isaac Watts's hymn *How Sweet and Awful Is the Place*:

Why was I made to hear thy voice,
    And enter while there's room,
When thousands make a wretched choice,
    And rather starve than come?

It wasn't until she became a parent that she began to see that in all salvation testimonies, it's not the outward circumstances that are amazing—it's the grace.

Even though Megan can't point to a specific day of spiritual awakening, she can point to her Lord who says, "All those the Father gives me will come to me, and whoever comes to me I will never drive away" (John 6:37). In response to that, Megan's prayer is "My Jesus, I come. Every day in need of grace. And I find myself not cast out."[6]

Everybody has a story, yet things aren't always as they seem. How you live, who and what you love, and how you deal with your sin is a far greater indicator of spiritual life than what you say or how you serve in the church.

> For we must all appear before the judgment seat of Christ, so that each of us may receive what is due us for what he has done while in the body, whether good or evil (2 Cor. 5:10).

God's judgment isn't based on outward appearance or on a profession of faith; it's based on the truth. John McArthur said in a sermon, "The hope of the hypocrite is that God will judge him by something else besides the truth."[7]

There'll be a great reveal in heaven someday, and when it comes, my prayer is that you will not hear the Lord Jesus speaking to you these seven words: "I never knew you, depart from me."

"For it is not the one who commends himself who is approved, but the one whom the Lord commends" (2 Cor. 10:18).

Remember

Someday there will be a great reveal in heaven when God identifies those who are truly his.

Ask Yourself

1. Can a person walk away from a genuine faith in Jesus?

2. What about Charo Washer's story was a surprise to you? Do you think she was mistaken in believing she wasn't a Christian?

3. What about Gary Shriver's testimony makes you think that he is, or isn't a Christian?

4. How can someone with a boring testimony know they are really a Christian since there is little change in their lifestyle?

5. Do you see God more as a loving father or as a righteous judge? How do you reconcile the two?

CHAPTER TWENTY

The Gospel Changes
Everything

Therefore, if anyone is in Christ, he is a new creation.
The old has passed away; behold, the new has come.
2 Corinthians 5:17

My husband Brad and I joined the Gideons sixteen years ago. The Gideons organization has been distributing Bibles for more than a hundred years, and is best known for placing Bibles in hotel rooms and fifth-grade classrooms. Their hotel Bibles have been used by God to bring many lost and desperate travelers to saving faith in the Lord Jesus Christ.

In recent years at the annual Gideon convention, one of the themes was "The Gospel Changes Everything." I like that statement, because it's so true. When someone accepts the good news of the gospel, their life is transformed.

An encounter with Jesus transformed the life of Saul of Tarsus from a zealous, Christian-hating Pharisee into the apostle Paul. When Saul met Jesus on the road to Damascus, he went from a Christian killer to someone who was ultimately killed for being a Christian.

As a Pharisee, he was completely devoted to the Jewish law. Upholding the law and seeing that it was upheld was of primary importance to him. To Saul, the law was the

191

way of salvation. The assertions by Christians that Jesus was the way to salvation robbed the law of its power and caused Saul to be hostile to both the message and the messengers.

When Saul finally accepted the message of the gospel, he experienced much more than a name change; he became Paul and was utterly transformed in both character and purpose in life. And this transformed Paul wrote these words to the church in Galatia: "A person is not justified by the works of the law, but through faith in Jesus Christ.... By works of the law no one will be justified" (Gal. 2:16).

Paul experienced much persecution during his life. He was flogged, beaten with rods, stoned, and ultimately martyred for the sake of Christ.

The Bible doesn't tell us about Paul's death, but Eusebius, an early church historian, stated that Paul was beheaded during the reign of Rome's Emperor Nero. As a Roman citizen, Paul was exempt from crucifixion, unlike some of the other apostles who were executed that way. Paul's martyrdom occurred shortly after much of Rome burned in a fire—an event that Nero blamed on the Christians.

From the inception of Christianity, the transformative power of the gospel has been evident, and it's still evident today.

A Life Set Free

William Scheremet believes in the power of testimony— which is why he tells his story of a life set free from addiction and hopelessness.

His first addiction was alcohol, which started with his first drink when he was just twelve years old at a sleepover.

From his first introduction to alcohol until the age of twenty-five, hardly a week went by without his getting drunk.

Bullied in elementary school, he got involved in all sorts of risky behavior to try to fit in. After drinking, he and his friends would at times go vandalizing in the neighborhood just for the thrill. When just nine or ten, he had an accidental introduction to pornography, the beginning of what would later become an addiction.

He loved the adrenaline rush from motocross, his favorite sport. In seventh grade, an accident left him with two shattered ankles. The pain was so bad that he was put on OxyContin. After the pain subsided, he pretended to still be hurting, to get more of the drug. His parents eventually figured out what was going on and cut him off, which led to a painful withdrawal period.

During high school, his life continued its downward spiral. By the time he reached college he was fully enslaved to alcohol, sex, pornography, and drugs. He experimented with many different kinds of drugs, including marijuana, ecstasy, mushrooms, and LSD.

During this period in his life, William called himself an atheist and would make fun of people who believed in God.

Shortly after William graduated from college, he was involved in a dirt bike collision while riding with a friend. William was instantly paralyzed. The pain was so great that he just wanted to die.

He was airlifted to the hospital. As he was being wheeled into the surgery room, he was told, "You might not make it." It was the last thing he remembers hearing before the surgery.

I guess this must be the end, he thought.

However, God wasn't finished with William.

During his recovery, he had lots of time to himself. Drugs, alcohol, and sex were stripped from his life, and he was left feeling empty and depressed.

He started reading self-help and new age books, thinking they might be the answer, but they weren't. One day he felt inclined to read the Bible. He downloaded a digital copy from the internet and started reading on page one. As he read, his heart started softening, and he became open to the idea that God exists.

One night he had a dream in which he was reliving a lot of the bad things he'd done. He sensed that he was being accused of these things, as if on trial, and he felt a heavy weight of guilt. It seemed as if demons were chasing him, and he was terrified.

Suddenly he was in a peaceful garden, bright and green. He saw a gravestone in the shape of a Celtic cross, with a bright light shining behind it. He went up to it and said, "Okay, God, I give up. I need the help of Jesus Christ."

The instant he said the name of Jesus, he felt a wave of cleansing, and he suddenly understood who Jesus was.

He woke up with a sense of excitement, wondering what had just happened. It was four in the morning, and he couldn't get back to sleep, so he picked up his Bible and started reading from where he'd left off in the book of Job.

> For God speaks in one way,
>> and in two, though man does not perceive it.
> In a dream, in a vision of the night,
>> when deep sleep falls on men,

while they slumber on their beds,
> then he opens the ears of men
and terrifies them with warnings,
> that he may turn man aside from his deed
and conceal pride from a man;
> he keeps back his soul from the pit,
his life from perishing by the sword (Job 33:14-18).

That's what just happened to me, he told himself. He understood that Jesus was real, and he began to weep. For the first time, he had hope.

Even though William is in a wheelchair today, he says his life is so much better. He began to pray that God would bring him friends and that he would find a church. God answered.

William is a new creation; his life has been completely and radically transformed. He says,

> God has transformed me in such a powerful way. He's real, and he made us for a purpose— to be with him, to praise him, to love him, and to love our neighbors.
>
> I'm just experiencing so much love right now; I just want to make Jesus known to people. I want people to see how he can change their lives, your life. That's why I'm sharing this story. Even the worst of people, the people who have done terrible, terrible things. No matter how far from God you are, Jesus can still heal you and transform you and give you new life. Turn to Jesus, read the Bible, just say a prayer—say, "Jesus, show up in my life, show me who you are," and he will show up, and it will be amazing for you.[1]

Seven Words You Never Want to Hear

William had been tormented and enslaved by sin and guilt for so long, but now God had set him free. He was freed from his porn addiction and has been sober since that day with no urge to use.

"It works," William said. "Just like the Bible says, he frees the captives."

Although William was freed instantly from his addictions, that isn't the experience of everyone who's born again. Many still experience a painful withdrawal period, as William had experienced earlier in his life with OxyContin. When I heard William's testimony, it appeared obvious to me that he'd been saved. The evidence was his transformed life. There are, however, some unconventional elements to his testimony, which made me wonder, What happened? At what point was he saved?

I share William's story with you to highlight the fact that it's all about the heart. God sees the intent of our hearts. We can't see another person's heart. We can't even know our own hearts. The prophet Jeremiah says, "The heart is deceitful above all things, and desperately sick; who can understand it?" (Jer. 17:9).

People like a formulaic prayer because it's simple and straightforward. Once someone has prayed a sinner's prayer, they're pronounced saved; it's a done deal. When someone comes to Jesus differently, we have questions.

God says, "This is the one to whom I will look: he who is humble and contrite in spirit and trembles at my word" (Isa. 66:2).

A few years ago, I shared the gospel with someone who'd heard it many times before that occasion. I said to him, "When you become a Christian, you won't have to tell me. I'll know."

The proof that God has done a work in someone's heart is that their life is transformed.

———✦———

After God saved a girl I'll call Ann, she began to get into God's Word and to attend an evangelical church. She became disillusioned and shocked as she saw her peers, who claimed to be Christians, participating in things that she'd just been saved from. Professing Christians were getting drunk, swearing, slandering one another, and sleeping with their boyfriends and girlfriends. The church kids knew all about Jesus but had never had their lives transformed by Jesus.

That old lifestyle had become repulsive to Ann as her love for Jesus and desire for holiness grew. How could people who claimed to love Jesus live that way? Although she was the new Christian and hadn't come from a Christian home, she knew she needed to look for direction from God's Word, not from people.

———✦———

The gospel changed the way Andrew Goud dealt with the lure of financial gain. While in his twenties, he entered into a business partnership with a friend, which began as a thrilling adventure. Andrew had come to know Jesus through a Bible correspondence course when he was twelve years old. His business partner was not a believer.

After a few years, Andrew began to feel uncomfortable in that business relationship as the two men had different moral standards. The closer Andrew drew to the Lord, the less content he felt in this business relationship. This resulted in Andrew taking a break from his work to give himself the space and time to reevaluate.

He took a full year off and traveled through the South Pacific and eventually Asia and Africa. A man who would later become his father-in-law encouraged him to consider a short-term mission trip. This led him to Papua New Guinea, where he was introduced to the work of New Tribes Mission (now called Ethnos). He was also introduced to Cathy, who would become his wife.

When Andrew returned to Canada, he knew the Lord was convicting him to dissolve his business partnership, which had been in place for about three years. By leaving the partnership Andrew relinquished his original investment of $50,000 plus other monies that would have been due him.

The Lord was also showing him where he should go next.

Andrew returned to Papua New Guinea. He and Cathy eventually married and have been working as missionaries among the remote Wusuraambya tribal people for almost thirty years.

When speaking of the financial loss, Andrew said,

> All of that meant nothing compared with the rewards of serving the One who saved me. Matthew 16:26 has often come to mind, which says, "For what will it profit a man if he gains the whole world and loses his own soul?" I was giving up something that could never satisfy in exchange for a ministry with eternal rewards. Lives would be changed forever. I would be changed forever! In Matthew 16:24-25, Jesus tells us to deny ourselves, to take up our cross

and follow Him. Serving the risen Savior comes with a price, but the eternal rewards far outweigh the sacrifice. Our lives are ever so brief and then eternity. What is the sacrifice of a few short years on earth compared to spending eternity with our Savior in Heaven? It's not as much a sacrifice as it is a privilege.[2]

I've shared stories of how God took people out of the kingdom of darkness and transformed their lives when they believed the gospel. The gospel changes not only our lifestyle and our priorities but also how we walk through trials in this life.

Once we've accepted the message of the gospel and are truly born again, we still have the choice of whether we'll trust God with our day-to-day circumstances. As believers, we can still succumb to fear rather than faith.

Earlier I mentioned joining the Gideons sixteen years ago. How we joined is a story of how God used something bad to bring about something good.

We were anticipating the birth of our first child, and my mother-in-law was baptized at age seventy-one -- life seemed good for Brad and me.

But on the day after her baptism, I began to bleed, and

I knew something wasn't right. My in-laws drove me to the hospital, where the examining doctor told me, "You're going to lose the baby."

I called my husband, Brad, and told him the news. I heard him weep on the other end of the telephone.

Although the doctor had predicted a grim outcome, the Orangeville Hospital sent me by ambulance to North York General Hospital in Toronto, which was the hospital where I was supposed to deliver the baby. When I arrived, they put me on antilabor drugs and did everything possible to keep me from having the baby early.

When Brad arrived, we prayed together, saying, "Lord, you know we want this baby, but your will be done."

For three days I remained in the hospital with my feet elevated while the doctors did everything medically possible to keep the baby from being born prematurely.

Finally, on October 25, 2001, God's will became known as I gave birth to a tiny baby boy. His little heart was beating as he arrived, but it slowly stopped beating as Brad held him in his arms.

We hadn't chosen a name for our child before his birth, but as we tried to decide on a name, the story of Hannah came to mind. She wanted a child and promised God that if he gave her one, she would give him back. When God gave her Samuel, she did as she'd promised and gave her son back to God.

We, too, had prayed for a child, and when God's will in this matter became clear, we felt as though we were giving our own son, whom we named Samuel, back to God. The pain at that moment was great, but the peace of God was greater.

That day I lived the words of verses I had quoted many times in my life:

> Don't worry about anything; instead, pray about everything. Tell God what you need, and thank him for all he has done. Then you will experience God's peace, which exceeds anything we can understand. His peace will guard your hearts and minds as you live in Christ Jesus (Phil. 4:6-7 NLT).

Never before in my life had I experienced such peace as I did then, even though I was walking through one of the greatest trials of my life. I can't fully describe how I felt, but the Bible clearly tells us that this peace God offers us will exceed anything we can understand.

I wanted to give Bibles to all the nurses who'd taken care of me during my time in the hospital, and the Gideons came to mind as a place to get Bibles. My mother made some inquiries for me and discovered that we needed to be Gideons in order to give out Gideon Bibles. Since we weren't Gideons at the time, I gave the nurses copies of the *Women's Devotional Bible.*

Realizing how great it would be to have a constant supply of Bibles, we later joined the Gideons. That decision, born out of sorrow, has given us the opportunity to witness and distribute God's Word on a scale we could never have imagined.

———————

You may be thinking, "I've never had that sort of peace amid trials." I understand how you feel, because I don't always get it right either. But the reward is great when we pray instead of worrying.

In her book *Jesus is Victor*, Corrie Ten Boom had a great analogy about worry. "When a train goes through a tunnel and it gets dark, you don't throw away the ticket and jump off. You sit still and trust the engineer."[3]

———

Our story doesn't end there. Not long after Samuel was born, I became pregnant again. It was discovered that I had an incompetent cervix, so to keep the baby from arriving early, the doctor stitched my cervix. Friends began to pray for us and for a safe arrival of the new life growing inside me. Although I had a stitch, which was the medical answer to my situation, we were trusting God, not the stitch.

During week twenty of this pregnancy, I began having labor pains, so we headed to the hospital. Not long after arriving, my water broke, and I knew the chances of this baby surviving were slim to none.

The next morning the nurse put the monitor on my belly looking for a heartbeat, and she found none. The baby had died during the night.

Such heartache—yet God did not disappoint; his comfort was great.

Strangely, I felt even more peace this time. I could easily have slipped into despair and hopelessness, yet I felt even greater confidence and trust in the Lord. So many people were praying for my pregnancy and the baby, yet God still chose to take our child home to himself. With all those prayers, I could come to only one conclusion: This was all part of God's plan. I trusted him and once again he rewarded that trust with peace. Again, it's impossible to describe what I experienced as I discovered the truth of God's promise to give us peace "which surpasses all understanding."

On the tombstone marking the place where our children are buried, we put this verse: "The LORD gave, and the LORD has taken away. Blessed be the name of the LORD" (Job 1:21).

My condition had prevented me from carrying even a tiny baby to full term, despite medical intervention. But by the grace and mercy of God, he eventually gave us a beautiful baby boy who weighed nine pounds, eleven ounces. What a blessing George Caleb was and is!

Three years later, God blessed us with his brother Josiah. God had so much more to teach us, as Josiah has Down syndrome. Those early days were especially difficult, but God was faithful as usual.

I was forty-one when Josiah was born, so statistically I had a one-in-forty chance of having a child with Down syndrome. Brad had a beautiful response to that statistic. He claimed our chances of having a child with Down syndrome were actually one hundred percent—because Josiah was the child God had for us. Nothing happens by chance!

———•———

Accepting the good news of the gospel changes everything in our lives. Like a caterpillar that has metamorphosed into a butterfly, we're a new creation. Our priorities, passions, and perspective are transformed. Old things have passed away, and all things have become new.

REMEMBER

The transformative power of the gospel is still evident today.

Ask Yourself

1. How did the power of the gospel change the life of Saul of Tarsus?

2. How have you been able to trust God in the everyday struggles of your life?

3. Think of an instance when God gave you peace in the middle of difficult circumstances.

4. Has the gospel changed your life? If so, how?

5. Use Scripture to back up your answer. What sort of changes will be evident in the life of a person who professes to be a Christian?

CHAPTER TWENTY-ONE

Nothing but the Truth

What is truth?
John 18:38

Post-truth was voted word of the year by *The Oxford English Dictionary* in 2016. Post-truth means "relating to or denoting circumstances in which objective facts are less influential in shaping public opinion than appeals to emotion and personal beliefs."[1]

A similar word, *truthiness*, was voted word of the year by the American Dialect Society in 2005. Popularized by Stephen Colbert on his satirical mock-news show *The Colbert Report*, it refers to "the quality of preferring concepts or facts one wishes to be true, rather than concepts or facts known to be true." Colbert jokingly put it this way: "I don't trust books. They're all fact, no heart."[2]

This book is based on the truth of God's Word. Jesus said, "If you abide in my word, you are truly my disciples, and you will know the truth, and the truth will set you free." This is not about judgment and condemnation but rather freedom and hope.

There will always be things in life that we wish were true even though they aren't. If something is true, it remains true whether or not I believe it to be true. Truth doesn't require my agreement. If I believe in error with enough sincerity, that doesn't turn error into truth.

One beautiful truth found throughout Scripture is that God is merciful and gracious. Grace and mercy are best understood as they relate to justice, which is getting what you deserve. Mercy means *not* getting what you deserve; grace means getting what you *don't* deserve.

An improper understanding of grace runs rampant in Christian circles. This is not a new problem. Paul addresses it in his letter to the Romans:

> What shall we say then? Are we to continue in sin that grace may abound? By no means! How can we who died to sin still live in it?…
>
> What then? Are we to sin because we are not under law but under grace? By no means! Do you not know that if you present yourselves to anyone as obedient slaves, you are slaves of the one whom you obey, either of sin, which leads to death, or of obedience, which leads to righteousness? (Rom. 6:1-2, 15-16).

Please take note of the end of verse 16. If you obey sin, you're headed toward death. But if your life is characterized by obedience to God's commands, that leads to righteousness.

Many falsely believe they're right with God, even though their actions show this is not the case. If you're saved, you won't live as you please, but your desire will be to live in a way that pleases God.

Our actions don't determine our destiny; they reveal it. Colin Smith expresses it this way:

> At the heart of Christ's kingdom stands the cross. And the cross is the place where grace and justice meet. Grace comes to us because justice was executed on Jesus.

It is not simply that God comes to those who believe and says, "I'll just sweep your sins under the carpet." No, God acts with justice when you come to faith in Jesus Christ, because justice is on Christ, so that in him grace and mercy, which reconciles you to God, may be released to you. Justice fell on him so that in him, the gift of grace may come to us.[3]

Spin is a word we hear thrown around today, especially in connection with news media or politicians. "To use spin is to manipulate meaning, to twist truth for particular ends—usually with the aim of persuading reader or listeners that things are other than they are."[4]

Many have spun the word *grace* to persuade themselves (and perhaps others) that as long as they believe in Jesus, they can live as they like.

God doesn't dispense his grace on a whim. In the spiritual realm, grace comes at a cost. Dietrich Bonhoeffer wrote this:

Cheap grace is the deadly enemy of our Church. We are fighting today for costly grace. Cheap grace means the justification of sin without the justification of the sinner. Grace alone does everything they say, and so everything can remain as it was before. "All for sin could not atone." Well, then let the Christian live like the rest of the world, let him model himself on the world's standards in every sphere of life, and not presumptuously aspire to live a different life under grace from his old life under sin.

Cheap grace is the preaching of forgiveness without requiring repentance…

Costly grace is the treasure hidden in the field; for the sake of it a man will gladly go and sell all that he has…. Such grace is costly because it calls us to follow, and it is grace because it calls us to follow Jesus Christ. It is costly because it costs a man his life, and it is grace because it gives a man the only true life. It is costly because it condemns sin and grace because it justifies the sinner.

Above all, it is costly because it costs God the life of His Son: "ye were bought at a price," and what has cost God much cannot be cheap for us.[5]

——————

The Bible makes it clear that all have sinned (Rom. 3:23) and that if we were to get what we deserved—justice— then we would get death (Rom. 6:23). We're all in the same boat, and that boat is sinking.

The Ten Commandments are part of the law that came through Moses. The law tells us what to do and what not to do but gives us no hope once we've broken it. We're incapable of keeping the law; it just reveals how sinful we really are.

Most people like to have a checklist so they know when they've completed necessary tasks. If the law is our checklist, we're in trouble, because we're incapable of fulfilling its requirements however hard we try. The law leaves us hopeless and helpless, since in our own strength it's impossible for us to live as God requires.

There is hope, however—but not through the law. Grace and truth came through Jesus Christ (John 1:18). Jesus doesn't just teach us the truth; he *is* the truth (John 14:6).

———

A few years ago, I clearly explained the gospel with a woman, and she really seemed to be getting it. She understood that she was a sinner, she appeared to understand what Christ had done on her behalf, and she seemed genuinely moved by the gospel's message.

In sharing the gospel, I'm leery of rushing someone into making a decision, and I usually encourage a person to go home and think about what they've heard. This time the woman seemed so ready that I asked her, "What are you going to do about what you heard today?"

Her response: "I'm going to try and not lie so much."

When I heard that, I was so glad I hadn't encouraged her to make a decision, since I realized that God still had some work to do in that woman's life. I once again explained to her that we can't earn our salvation. I gave her a New Testament and said goodbye, while praying that in God's time the seed that was planted would grow.

Despite a clear presentation of the gospel in which I'd explained that our good works wouldn't earn us favor with God, she still felt it was up to her to try harder. I hope that isn't the takeaway that you, my reader, have from this book.

I've outlined from Scripture certain activities and behaviors that aren't consistent with a person who professes faith. If you've been convicted about a particular area in your life, God isn't asking you to pull up your bootstraps and try harder. He's asking you to surrender your life to him. He doesn't want your best effort; he wants you to give up trying. The reality is that you can't do it in your own strength.

Justin Martyr, a Christian apologist of the second century, wrote of the difference faith in the Lord Jesus makes in a person's life:

> Those who once delighted in fornication now embrace chastity alone; we who once took most pleasure in accumulating wealth and property now…share with everyone in need; we who hated and killed one another and would not associate with men of different tribes because of their different customs now, since the coming of Christ live familiarly with them and pray for our enemies.[6]

A correct understanding of the facts of the gospel without a change in behavior reveals that there's no spiritual life. "Faith by itself, if it does not have works, is dead" (James 2:17).

While a change in lifestyle is evidence of saving faith, correct living without a changed heart makes you no better than the Pharisees.

To reject a clear command of Scripture is to reject God himself. I'll quote this verse again: "Let God be true, and every human being a liar" (Rom. 3:4).

In 2 Thessalonians 2:10, Paul speaks of "those who are perishing, because they refused to love the truth and so be saved."

It's popular today to speak of "my truth" and "your

truth." Our world has become so politically correct that it's offensive to speak of *the* truth.

> People are entitled to their own beliefs, but not their own truth. Belief is not what ultimately matters—truth is…. The bottom line is that we discover truth; we don't create it.[1]

God's truth is made clear in God's Word.

It is tragic to me to think that someone who knows the gospel and believes themselves to be saved will someday hear those seven words that nobody wants to hear: "I never knew you; depart from me."

The great desire of my heart is that everyone I know and love will come to know Jesus as Lord and Savior. May your heart and mine be broken by the things that break the heart of God. When that happens and you embrace the truth, it will lead to a changed life, and you can look forward to Jesus greeting you with seven words you truly want to hear: "Come…inherit the kingdom prepared for you" (Matt. 25:34).

The choice is yours.

REMEMBER

Our performance doesn't determine our destiny—it reveals it.

Ask Yourself

1. Do you believe in absolute truth? Why or why not?

2. When confronted with the truth, either in God's Word or from another person, are you more likely to let the truth change you, or do you spin the truth?

3. Do you love the truth? If so, how do you demonstrate that in your life?

4. Do you believe in cheap grace or costly grace? Please explain your answer.

5. What are you going to do about what you've read in this book?

"Flee from the Wrath to Come"

A Sermon by Charles H. Spurgeon

Who warned you to flee from the wrath to come?
Matthew 3:7

While researching for the chapter on the wrath of God, I came upon the following excellent sermon delivered by Charles Haddon Spurgeon at the Metropolitan Tabernacle in London on October 23, 1881. I had intended to quote only the parts that stood out to me, until I realized that it all stood out to me, so I decided in the end to include the sermon in its entirety. By the way, Spurgeon's collected sermons fill sixty-three volumes, and are currently the largest set of books by a single author in the history of Christianity.[1]

We will first consider the question of John the Baptist: "When he saw many of the Pharisees and Sadducees come to his baptism, he said unto them, O generation of vipers, who has warned you to flee from the wrath to come?" I have no doubt that the Pharisees and

Sadducees were very much surprised to hear John addressing them in that way; for men, who wish to win disciples, ordinarily adopt milder language than that, and choose more attractive themes, for they fear that they will drive their hearers from them if they are too personal, and speak too sharply.

There is not much danger of that nowadays, for the current notion now abroad is that gospel ministers can sew with silk without using a sharp needle; and that, instead of piercing men with the sword of the Spirit, they should show them only the hilt of it; let them see the bright diamonds on the scabbard, but never let them feel the sharpness of the two-edged blade! They should always comfort, and console, and cheer, but never allude to the terror of the Lord.

That appears to be the common interpretation of our commission; but John the Baptist was of quite another mind. There came to him a Pharisee, a very religious man, one who observed all the details of external worship, and was very careful even about trifles, a firm believer in the resurrection, and in angels and spirits, and in all that was written in the book of the law, and also in all the traditions of his fathers, a man who was overdone with external religiousness, a ritualist of the first order, who felt that if there was a righteous man in the world, he certainly was that one.

He must have been greatly taken aback when John talked to him about the wrath of God and plainly told him that that wrath was as much for him as for other people. Those phylacteries and the broad borders of his garment, of which he was so proud, would not screen him from the anger of God against injustice and transgression, but just like any common sinner, he would need to "flee from the wrath to come."

I daresay that the Sadducee was equally taken aback by John's stern language. He too was a religious man, but he combined with his religion greater thoughtfulness than the Pharisee did—at least, so he said. He did not believe in traditions; he was too large-minded to care about the little details and externals of religion. He observed the Law of Moses, but he clung rather to the letter of it than to its spirit, and he did not accept all that was revealed, for he denied that there was such a thing as an angel or a spirit. He was a Broad Churchman, a man of liberal ideas, fully abreast of the age. He professed to be a Hebrew of the Hebrews, yet at the same time the yoke of religion rested very lightly upon his shoulders. Still, he was not irreligious. Yet here is John the Baptist talking to him, as well as to the Pharisee, about "the wrath to come."

They would both have liked to have a little argument with him, but he talked to them about fleeing from the wrath to come. They would both have been pleased to discuss with him some theological questions, and to bring up the differences between their two sects, just to hear how John would handle them, and to let them see which way he would lean. But he did not waste a moment over the matters in dispute between Pharisees and Sadducees; the one point he had to deal with was the one of which he would have spoken to a congregation of publicans and harlots, and he spoke of it in just the same way to these nominally religious people. They must "flee from the wrath to come," or else as surely as they were living men, that wrath would come upon them, and they would perish under it.

So John just kept to that one topic. He laid the axe to the root of the trees as he warned these hypocritical professors to escape for their lives, otherwise they would perish in the common destruction which will overwhelm all ungodly men. This was not the style of preaching that John's hearers liked, but John did not think of that. He did not come to say what men wished him to say, but to discharge the burden of the Lord, and to speak out plainly what was best for men's eternal and immortal interests. Therefore he spoke first concerning the wrath of God, and next he spoke concerning the way of escape from that wrath.

Those shall be our two topics also. First, the tremendous peril: "the wrath to come"; and secondly, the means of escape: "Flee from the wrath to come."

First, dear friends, let us think of THE TREMENDOUS PERIL which overtakes all men who do not escape from it. That tremendous peril is the wrath of God. There is a wrath of God which abides on every ungodly man. Whether men like that truth or not, it is written, "God is angry with the wicked every day"; and also, "He that believes not is condemned already, because he has not believed in the name of the only begotten Son of God"; and yet again, "He that believes not the Son shall not see life; but the wrath of God abides on him."

But this wrath is in abeyance for a time, and consequently men do not think much either of the wrath that now is or of "the wrath to come." It will not, however, always be in abeyance. The sluices of the great deep will be pulled up, and the awful torrents will come leaping forth, and will utterly overwhelm all who are exposed to their fury. This "wrath to come" will in part fall upon men at death, but more fully at the Day of Judgment, and it will continue to flow over them forever and ever. This "wrath to come" is that of which John spoke, and of which we will now think for a while.

I remark first that this "wrath to come" is absolutely just and necessary. If there is a God, He cannot let sin go unpunished. If He is really God and the Judge of all the earth, He must have an utter abhorrence of all evil. It cannot be possible that He should think the same of the honest and the dishonest, of the chaste and the unchaste, of the sober and the drunken, of the truthful and the lying, of the gracious and the dissolute. Such a god as that would be one whom men might rightly despise. But the true God, if we understand aright what He is, must detest all sin. All evil must be utterly abhorrent to His pure and holy soul. And it is not only because He can do it, but because He must do it, that He will, one of these days, let loose the fury of His wrath against sin.

As it is necessary in the very nature of things that there should be certain laws to govern His creation, so is it equally necessary in the very nature of things that sin should be punished, and that every transgression and disobedience should receive a just recompense of reward. This is the inevitable consequence of sin. There is nothing arbitrary about such a result. It is fixed in the very nature of things that "for every idle word that men shall speak, they shall give account in the Day of Judgment," and for every sinful action they must appear before the bar of God.

Do not think when we speak about the wrath of God that we picture God as a tyrant. This is only the nature of things. Just as if you take poison it will kill you, or if you indulge in drunkenness or take almost any form of disease, it will bring pain and mischief to you— so sin must bring upon you the wrath of God. It cannot be otherwise. Heaven and earth shall pass away, but not one jot or tittle of God's law can pass away till all is fulfilled, and one part of that law requires that He should punish all transgression, iniquity, and sin.

And if now, for a time, the full manifestation of

that anger is delayed, I beseech you, men and brethren, do not therefore trifle with it. The longer God's arm is uplifted, the more terrible will be the blow when at last He strikes. To sin against the patience and long-suffering of Almighty God is to sin with a vengeance. You do, as it were, defiantly put your finger into the very eye of God when you know that He sees you sin, and yet you go on sinning because He does not immediately take vengeance upon you for all your evil works. It is in great love that He restrains His wrath, for He is "slow to anger, and plenteous in mercy." But as a torrent that is dammed up for a while gathers force and strength, and every hour in which it is kept back it gets to be more irresistible, so must it be with "the wrath to come" when at last it does come upon you. If it has waited for some of you for seventy, or sixty, or fifty, or even for twenty years, it will come as an overwhelming flood when at last it bursts the barriers which at present hold it back. Trifle not therefore with that long-suffering of God which may be blest to your salvation.

Nor is "the wrath to come" any the less sure because it is delayed. Because sentence is not at once given against an evil work, therefore men say, "We need not trouble ourselves. How does God know? And is there knowledge in the Most High? Behold, He winks at our iniquities. He counts them as mere trifles. No harm will come to us because of them." If you are prepared to cast away the Bible, I can understand a little that you should talk like that.

But if you really believe that the Scriptures are the Word of God, you know what the consequences of your sin must be. Concerning the wicked, it is written, "If he turns not, He will whet His sword; He has bent His bow, and made it ready. He has also prepared for him the instruments of death."

Even if you are so foolish as to cast away your Bibles, yet unless you think yourselves to be mere dogs and cattle that shall rot back into the ground from where you came and be done with forever, you must expect that there will be another state of existence in which right shall be vindicated and wrong shall be punished. It seems to lie upon the very conscience of man, in the unwritten code of intuitive knowledge, or of knowledge handed down from father to son, that there must come a time in which God will surely bring every secret thing to light, and visit with judgment the proud and the high-handed oppressor, and vindicate the rights of men and the rights of His own throne. It must be so. And if the wrath tarries for a while, it is nonetheless sure.

I feel quite staggered as I try to speak of this "wrath to come." When it does come, it must be something very terrible, because Divinity enters into the essence of it. The wrath of man is sometimes very terrible, but what must the wrath of God be?

I have tried these many years to preach the love of God humbly yet earnestly, and I have never yet reached the height of that great argument, for His love is boundless. But so are all His attributes; and if you consider any one of them, you must say, "It is high, I cannot attain unto it." But the just indignation of God against sin must be commensurate with His absolute purity. That man who trifles with right and wrong and thinks that these are mere arbitrary terms has no indignation when he sees wrong done. But God, who is infinitely pure and holy, cannot look upon sin without an awful abhorrence. It is not possible that He should. "Oh," He says, by the mouth of His servant Jeremiah, "do not do this abominable thing that I hate." He is not indifferent to sin, but He hates it, and He pleads with men not to do it because it is so abominable and so hateful in His sight.

What will "the wrath to come" be? If God but touches a man with only His little finger, as it were, the strongest must at once fail and fall, the mightiest can scarcely open his eyes, and the seal of death is speedily imprinted on his brow. But what will it be when the hand of God shall begin to plague the ungodly, when He shall pour out all the vials of His wrath upon them, and crush them with the bosses of His buckler? What will be their portion when He says, "Ah, I will ease Me of My adversaries, and avenge Me of My enemies?" Think too what must be the meaning of that terrible passage—let me repeat it to you slowly and solemnly— "Now consider this, you that forget God, lest I tear you in pieces, and there be none to deliver."

Thus have I faithfully tried to set before you "the wrath to come." Now listen to me for a few minutes, and let me have your impartial judgments, while I still further speak upon this important theme. Who do you think are the more honest men—those who tell you plainly what the Scriptures say concerning this wrath of God, or those who smooth it over or deny it altogether? I will not judge them; before the Judge of the quick and the dead let those appear who dare to be apologists for sin, and to diminish the dread thought of God's anger against it. Without any breach of Christian charity I might be permitted to suspect the honesty of those who use flattering words to please and deceive their hearers, but I could not suspect the honesty of those who preach an unpalatable truth which grieves themselves as much as it is distasteful to those who hear it.

Let me also ask you which style of preaching has the greater moral effect upon yourself. Will you be likely to go and sin after you have heard of God's anger against it, or will you more readily commit iniquity when you have it salved over, and you are told that it is but a little thing of which God takes no account?

I was in the cabin of a vessel one day with a brother minister who was disputing with me upon the non-eternity of future punishment. The captain of the ship came in and said, "What are you discussing down here? The scenery is beautiful, come up on deck and admire it." So I said to him, "This is the question in dispute:

whether the punishment of sin is eternal, or not." "Well," he said, "we cannot have any theological discussion just now." Turning to my opponent, he said, "Don't you go on deck and talk to my sailors any of your rubbish. They are bad enough as they are; but if you tell them what I heard you say just now, they will swear and drink worse than ever." Then, turning to me, he said, "You may talk to the men as much as you like; you will do them good and not harm by telling them that God will certainly punish their sins."

Now, there is common sense in that argument of my friend; you know that there is. That which is most likely to do good and to repress sin is most likely to be right, but that which gives me latitude to offend my conscience leads me to suspect whether it could ever have come from God at all, and makes me seriously doubt whether it can be true.

And what will be the consequence if it should turn out that we are mistaken when we preach to you concerning the wrath of God? What losers will those of us be who have fled to Christ for refuge? But suppose it should turn out that we are right—where will you be who have despised the wrath of God? We have two strings to our bow, but to my mind you have none at all. I would not like to lie down upon my deathbed in the hope that death would be an eternal sleep; that would be a miserable hope even if it could ever be fulfilled. I would not like to risk my destiny in the world to come upon the prospect of being annihilated because I was an unbeliever. It would be a wretched thing to hope for, but what if even that poor hope should fail me? Where should I be then? But I can go with confidence before my God and say to Him, "Be Your wrath what it may—I know that it must be terrible to the last degree—but be it what it may, I will not dare it; and even if it would not hurt me, yet I would not make You angry, O God, by sinning against You. And if there were no punishment for sin but the loss of Your love, if there were nothing but the loss of heaven, the loss of having failed to please You, my God, I would count that loss to be tremendous and terrible. Let me be reconciled to You, my Maker. Tell me how You can be just and yet forgive the guilty. To You I fly. Oh, save me from the wrath to come!"

Thus have I set before you, as best I can, the tremendous peril.

Now, in the second place, I want, for a few minutes, to tell you about THE MEANS OF ESCAPE. John said to the Pharisees and Sadducees, "Who has warned you to flee from the wrath to come?"

By this question, he seemed to imply that there is no way of deliverance from "the wrath to come" but by flight. Sinner, you cannot endure the wrath of God. If your ribs were granite, and your nerves were brass, you could not endure the wrath of the Almighty—no, not even for a moment. If a man had a toothache, how dreadful it would seem to him to have to bear that pain for twelve months for certain, even if he knew that there would be an end to it then. But what must the anger of God be when He comes to deal with our entire manhood, and to punish our sins forever and ever? We cannot bear it; we must flee from it. What does this mean?

It means, first, immediate action. You must escape. If you remain where you now are, you will certainly perish. You are in the City of Destruction which is to be overwhelmed with the fiery flood of "the wrath to come." You must be in earnest to escape from it before judgment is executed upon the place, and all who are in it. You must "flee from the wrath to come."

Fleeing means not only immediate action, but swift action. He that flees for his life does not creep and crawl; he runs at his utmost speed, and he wishes that he could ride on the wings of the wind. No pace that he can reach is fast enough for him. Oh, if God the Holy Spirit will make you feel your imminent danger, you will want to fly to Christ with the swiftness of a flash of lightning. You will not be satisfied to linger as you are even for another hour. What if that gallery should fall about your ears? What if God should smite the house while you are still in your sins? What if, in walking home, you should walk into your graves? What if your beds should become your tombs? It may be so with any one of you. So there is no time to linger or delay. Haste is the word for you. God sends it to you, and says, "Today if you will hear His voice, harden not your hearts"; "Behold, now is the accepted time; behold, now is the day of salvation."

To flee also means to go straight away at your objective. A man who flees for his life does not want any circuitous, roundabout roads. He takes shortcuts; he goes over hedge and ditch that he may get where he wants to be in the shortest possible space of time. So straight away to Jesus is the only direction for you just now. Some people will recommend you to read books, which I am certain you cannot understand, for no living soul can. Or perhaps you may meet with persons who want to explain to you some wondrous mystery. Listen to them, if you like, at the Day of Judgment when the great business of your salvation is over, but just now you have not any time for mysteries, you have no time for puzzlements, you have no time to be confused and confounded. The one thing you have to do is to go straightaway to Jesus, straightaway to Jesus. You are a sinner, and He is the only Savior for sinners, so trust Him. God help you to trust Him, and thus to find immediate salvation! It is a straight road to Christ. The plan of salvation is not a thing that is hard to be understood. "He that believes on the Son has everlasting life," and he shall never come into condemnation; for he as passed from death unto life. There is the gospel in a nutshell. Lay hold of it, and live by it. You have not time for anything else, and you have no need of anything else. So flee, "flee from the wrath to come."

Notice how John the Baptist explained to those Pharisees and Sadducees the way in which they had to flee. He told them first that they must repent. There is no going to heaven by following the road to hell. There is no finding pardon while continuing in sin. Depend upon it, Mr. Drunkard; you will not be forgiven for your drunkenness if you still go on with your drinking. Let not the man who is unchaste imagine that he can go on with his sin and yet be forgiven. Let not the thief dream that there is any pardon for him unless he quits his evil course, and tries to make such restitution as he can to those whom he has wronged.

There must be repentance, then, and that repentance must be practical. Note how John put it: "Bring forth, therefore, fruits meet for repentance"—evidences of true amendment of life. It is no use whining and crying and going into the inquiry rooms with a lie in your right hand, and then going home to swear and drink or to break the Sabbath, and to live as you like, and all the while hoping to enter heaven. No, sin and you must part, or else Christ and you can never keep company.

You remember the message that John Bunyan thought he heard when he was playing at tip-cat on a Sunday on the village green? He suddenly stood still with the stick in his hand, for he thought he heard a voice saying to him, "Will you leave your sins, and go to heaven, or have your sins, and go to hell?" That is the alternative which both the law and the gospel put before men. "Flee from the wrath to come"—but there is no fleeing from wrath except by repentance of sin, and by fruits meet for repentance, evidences of a real change of heart and life.

Then John went on to say to the Pharisees and Sadducees that they must give up all the false hopes which they had cherished: "Think not to say within yourselves, We have Abraham as our father." Those Pharisees said, in deed if not in word, "It really does not matter though we act the hypocrite, for Abraham is our father." And the Sadducees said in effect, "Though we are unbelievers, it is of small consequence, for Abraham is our father." "No," answered John, "you must abandon all such false hopes as that."

And if any of you, dear friends, have said, "We shall be all right, because we are regular church people;" or if you have said, "We are all right, for we are Baptists, we are Methodists, we are Presbyterians; our father and mother and our grandfather and grandmother were good Christian people." Ah, yes! And so may your great grandfather and great grandmother have been, but your pedigree will avail you nothing unless you personally quit your sins and lay hold on Christ as your Savior. Nor is there anything else upon which you can depend for salvation. Your baptism, your churchgoing, your chapel going, your eating of the Lord's Supper, your saying of collects, your family prayers, your giving of your guineas, everything of your own put together will all be less than nothing and vanity if you trust to it. You must flee away from all such false hopes as that, and get a better hope, even that of which my second text speaks: "That by two immutable things, in which it was impossible for God to lie, we might have a strong consolation, who have fled for refuge to lay hold upon the hope set before us."

John the Baptist did not tell his hearers all this, for he did not come to preach the gospel to them. He came to preach the law, but he did sufficiently indicate where they must go, for he said to them, "There stands one among you whom you know not.… He shall baptize you with the Holy Spirit, and with fire." It is to Him, even to Jesus, that you must flee. If you would be saved, you must be among those who have fled for refuge to lay hold upon the hope set before you. That is the real refuge for sinners—the laying hold of Christ, the getting a faith-grip of Jesus as the one atoning sacrifice, the looking to Him with tearful but believing eyes and saying, "Jesus, Son of God, I trust in You; I put myself into Your hands, and leave myself there, that You may deliver me from the wrath to come."

I pray you, brethren and sisters, wherever you are, you who think you are so good, be anxious to get rid of all that fancied goodness of yours. I beseech you, if you have any self-righteousness about you, to ask God to strip it off you at once. I should like you to feel as that man did who had a forged bank note and some counterfeit coin in his possession. When the policeman came to his house, he was anxious not to have any of it near him. So shake off your self-righteousness. You will be as surely damned by your righteousness, if you trust in it, as you will by your unrighteousness. Christ alone, the gift of the free grace of God—this is the gate of heaven. But all self-satisfaction, all boasting, all exaltation of yourself above your fellow men is mischievous and ruinous, and will surely be deadly to your spirit forever.

How does Christ deliver us from "the wrath to come"? Why, by putting Himself into our place, and putting us into His place. Oh, this blessed plan of salvation by substitution! That Christ should take a poor guilty sinner and set him up there in the place of acceptance and joy at the right hand of God, and that, in order to be able to do so, Christ should say, "Here comes the great flood of almighty wrath; I will stand just where it is coming, and let it flow over Me." And you know that it did flow over Him till He sweat, as it were, great drops of blood, and more, till He cried aloud, "My God, My God why have You forsaken Me?" And still more, till He cried, "It is finished," and He bowed His head, and gave up the ghost— "He bore, that you might never bear, His Father's righteous ire." And so, suffering in your stead, and putting you into the place of acceptance which He Himself so well deserves to occupy, He saved you from "the wrath to come."

I used to think that if I once told this wondrous story of "free grace and dying love," everybody would believe it. But I have long since learned that so hard is the heart of man, that he will sooner be damned than be saved by Christ. Well, you must make your choice. You must make your choice for yourselves. Only do me this one favor, when you have made your choice: Do not blame me for having tried to persuade you to act more wisely than I fear your choice will be. I sometimes tremble as I think of the account I have to give concerning the many thousands who crowd this place to listen to my voice.

What if my Master should say to me, at the last, "You flattered them; you tried to run with the times; you did not dare to preach to them the old-fashioned gospel, and to tell them of hell and of judgment and of atonement by blood"? No, my Master, You will never be able to say that to me. With all my faults and infirmities and imperfections, I have sought to declare Your truth, as far as I knew it, to the sons of men.

Therefore, my hearers, I shake my skirts free of your blood. If any of you shall reject Christ, I will have nothing to do with your damnation. Be spiritual suicides if you will. But I will not be your soul-murderer, nor act like Saul wished his armor-bearer to do when he bade him thrust him through with the sword. I implore you to "flee from the wrath to come." Escape by quitting your sins and laying hold on Jesus, and do it this very moment, for you may never have another opportunity to do it. May the Lord in His infinite mercy grant you grace to trust in Jesus! Amen and Amen.

Notes

Introduction: So Much at Stake

1 Penn Gillette, "A Gift of a Bible," *Penn Says* podcast, aired on July 8, 2010, YouTube video, https://www.youtube.com/watch?v=6md638s-mQd8.

2 Amy Carmichael, letter to a fellow author, quoted in Frank L. Houghton, *Amy Carmichael of Dohnavur* (Fort Washington, PA: CLC Publications, 1979), 364.

Chapter One: The Christian Home Syndrome

1 Paul Washer, "Examine Yourself," sermon given at Grace Community Church, San Antonio, Texas, May 11, 2009.

Chapter Two: How Jesus Evangelized

1 Mishnah, Tractate Shabbat 7:2.

2 This section is the author's adaptation of content from *Pilgrimage from Rome* by Bartholomew F. Brewer with Alfred W. Furrell (Greenville, SC: Bob Jones University Press, 1982, 1986).

3 Second Vatican Council, "Dogmatic Constitution on Divine Revelation," no. 9. According to the Second Vatican Council: "The Church does not draw her certainty about all revealed truths from the holy Scriptures alone. Hence, both Scripture and Tradition must be accepted and honored with equal feelings of devotion and reverence."

Chapter Three: Follow Me

1 *Biography*, A & E Entertainment Channel, June 6, 2018.

2 Jonathan N. Daugherty, "Discipleship is Jewish," Heart of God Israel, a ministry of Heart of God International. https://heartofgodisrael.org/messianic-messages/discipleship-is-jewish/.

3 *The Mishnah,* Avot 2, translated by Herbert Danby (Oxford: Oxford University Press, 1933).

4 *The Mishnah,* Avot 5:21.

5 *The Mishnah,* Bava Metsi'a 2:11.

6 Doug Greenwold, *Making Disciples Jesus' Way: Wisdom We Have Missed* (Gaithersburg, Maryland: Signature Book Printing, Inc.).

7 Hillel (10 B.C.–A.D. 10) and Shimmai (50 B.C.–A.D. 30) were Jewish scholars and sages.

8 Francis Chan, *Multiply: Disciples Making Disciples* (Colorado Springs: David C. Cook, 2012).

9 Doug Greenwold, *Making Disciples Jesus' Way*, A Digging Deeper Faith Study (Douglas J. Greenwold, 2007), 23.

Chapter Five: Repentance—the Missing Note

1 H. A. Ironside, *Except Ye Repent* (Grand Rapids: Baker, 1960).

2 Ray Comfort, "Way of the Master" video, Basic Training Course, Living Waters Publications, 2014.

3 A. W. Tozer, *The Root of the Righteous* (Camp Hill, Pennsylvania: Christian Publications, 1986), 42–43.

Chapter Six: Strange Fruit

1 Dorian Lynskey, *33 Revolutions per Minute* (Faber & Faber, Ltd., 2011). From extract published as "Strange Fruit: The first great protest song" in *The Guardian,* February 16, 2011; https://www.theguardian.com/music/2011/feb/16/protest-songs-billie-holiday-strange-fruit.

2 "2014 State of Dating in America," Christian Mingle & Date.

3 Charles Spurgeon, "The Lesson of the Almond Tree," Sermon 2678, April 7, 1881. Accessed at http://www.spurgeongems.org/vols46-48/chs2678.pdf.

Chapter Seven: Confession

1 *Strong's New Testament*, 3670: *homologeo.*

2 Swindoll, Charles, *David: A Man of Passion and Destiny* (Nashville: Thomas Nelson, 2000), 10–11.

3 "Lance Armstrong: key quotes from Oprah interview," *The Telegraph*, December 23, 2019.https://www.telegraph.co.uk/sport/othersports/cycling/lancearmstrong/9810203/Lance-Armstrong-key-quotes-from-Oprah-interview.html.

4 Paul H. B. Shin, "Lance Armstrong on Doping: 'I Would Probably Do It Again," ABC News, January 26, 2019. https://abcnews.go.com/Sports/lance-armstrong-doping/story?id=28491316.

5 Tim Baysinger, "Felicity Huffman to Plead Guilty in College Admissions Cheating Case," *The Wrap*, MSN, April 9, 2019. https://www.msn.com/en-ca/entertainment/celebrity/felicity-huffman-to-plead-guilty-in-college-admissions-cheating-case/ar-BBVKpVB.

6 "Clergyman Confesses Adultery, Resigns," *Washington Post*, 1987. https://www.washingtonpost.com/archive/local/1987/06/13/clergyman-confesses-adultery-resigns/c90a8281-db18-4b9e-887a-878d628ba75a/.

Chapter Eight: Forgiveness

1 Craig Parro, "A Testimony that Reminds Us Why We Do What We Do," *Leadership Resources*, August 8, 2019.

2 Oswald Chambers, James Reimann, ed., *My Utmost for His Highest* (Grand Rapids: Discovery House, 1992), November 20.

3 Corrie ten Boom with Elizabeth Sherrill, John Sherrill, *The Hiding Place* (Grand Rapids: Chosen Books), 1971.

4 *The Dallas Morning News*, Oct. 02, 2019. YouTube video, https://www.bing.com/videos/search?q=brandt+jean+statement&&view=detail&mid=CCDAE212CC32A57A8604CCDAE212CC32A57A8604&&FORM=VRDGAR.

5 Whoopi Goldberg, *The View*, ABC, October 3, 2019.

6 John Piper, interview episode 669, August 24, 2015.

Chapter Nine: Examine Your Obedience

1 John Piper, sermon "Command of God: The Obedience of Faith," Dec. 8, 2008.

2 Piper, "Command of God: The Obedience of Faith."

Chapter Ten: Examine Your Loves

1 John Wesley, quoted at Goodreads, https://www.goodreads.com/quotes/349175-what-one-generation-tolerates-the-next-generation-will-embrace.

2 Dietrich Bonhoeffer, quoted at Goodreads, https://www.goodreads.com/author/quotes/29333.Dietrich_Bonhoeffer.

3 Martin Luther, quoted at Goodreads, https://www.goodreads.com/quotes/346054-next-to-the-word-of-god-music-deserves-the-highest.

4 Tom Waitts, quoted at Goodreads, https://www.goodreads.com/quotes/123516-i-like-beautiful-melodies-telling-me-terrible-things.

5 J. S. Strouse, N. Buerkel-Rothfuss, E. C. Long, "Gender and family as moderators of the relationship between music video exposure and adolescent sexual permissiveness," *Adolescence,* 1995; 30 (119): 505–521. Also L. E. Greeson, R. A. Williams, "Social implications of music videos

for youth: an analysis of the content and effects of MTV," *Youth Soc,* 1986; 18 (2):177–189.

6 J. D. Brown, K. L. L'Engle, C. J. Pardum, G. J. Guo, K. Kenneavy, C. Jackson, "Sexy media matter: exposure to sexual content in music, movies, television, and magazines predicts black and white adolescents' sexual behavior," *Pediatrics,* 2006; 117 (4):1018–1027.

7 K. L. L'Engle, J. D. Brown, K. Kenneavy, "The mass media are an important context for adolescents' sexual behavior," *J. Adolescent Health*, 2006; 38 (3):186–192.

8 S. Knobloch-Westerwick, P. Musto, K. Shaw, "Rebellion in the top music charts: defiant messages in rap/hip hop and rock music—1993–2003," presented at: The International Communication Association Conference; Dresden, Germany, June 19–23, 2006.

9 Opening lines (slightly edited) from "Freebase" source definition given at Definitions.net; https://www.definitions.net/definition/modesty.

10 Robert Murray McCheyne, *Memoir and Remains of the Rev. Robert Murray McCheyne,* (Edinburgh, 1894), 293.

11 John Piper, *Future Grace* (Colorado Springs: Multnomah, 2005), 329.

Chapter Eleven: Dying to Self

1 Dietrich Bonhoeffer, *The Cost of Discipleship* (New York: Touchstone, 1995), 99.

2 Roger Steer, *George Mueller: Delighted in God* (Fearn, Tain, Ross-shire, Scotland, UK: Christian Focus Publications, 1997).

3 Jerry Bridges, *The Discipline of Grace*, as quoted by Tim Challies in @ Challies, "If We Have Died to Sin, Why Do We Still Sin?" blogpost, Aug. 30, 2012. https://www.challies.com/reading-classics-together/if-we-have-died-to-sin-why-do-we-still-sin/.

Chapter Twelve: Those Who Counted the Cost

1 John Foxe, *Foxe's Book of Martyrs*, "The Bamboo Curtain" (Alachua, FL.: Bridge-Logos, 1969) pp. 329–330.

2 *Foxe's Book of Martyrs*, 413.

3 Richard Wurmbrand, "Tortured for Christ," in *A Ready Defense*, Josh McDowell (Nashville: Thomas Nelson, 1993), 440–441.

4 Paul Washer, sermon "Examine Yourself," Grace Community

Church, San Antonio, Texas, May 11, 2009. www.GCCSATX.com.

5 Amy Carmichael, "Hast Thou No Scar?" in *Mountain Breezes: The Collected Poems of Amy Carmichael* (Fort Washington, PA: CLC Publications, 1999), 173.

6 Rosaria Champagne Butterfield, *The Secret Thoughts of an Unlikely Convert: An English Professor's Journey into Christian Faith* (Pittsburgh: Crown & Covenant Publications, 2014), 21.

7 Butterfield, *Secret Thoughts,* 21.

Chapter Thirteen: The Gospel of Greed

1 See 1 Corinthians 6:9–10; Galatians 5:19–21; Ephesians 5; Romans 2:1–16; Revelation 22.

2 Costi Hinn, *God, Greed, and the Prosperity Gospel* (Grand Rapids: Zondervan, 2019), 15.

3 Hinn, *God, Greed, and the Prosperity Gospel,* 46.

4 Richard N. Ostling, *Time* magazine article, July 13, 1987.

5 https://www.latimes.com/archives/la-xpm-1987-04-02-mn-1975-story.html

6 Edwin Harrell Jr., *Oral Roberts: An American Life* (Bloomington, Indiana: Indiana University Press), from the book jacket.

7 Hinn, *God, Greed, and the Prosperity Gospel,* 155.

8 https://www.bbc.com/news/stories-47675301.

9 https://www.christianpost.com/news/televangelist-creflo-dollar-needs-200000-people-to-donate-300-each-so-he-can-buy-65m-ministry-plane-135582/.

10 https://www.cnn.com/2018/05/30/us/jesse-duplantis-plane-falcon-7x-prosperity-gospel-trnd/index.html.

11 https://www.insideedition.com/investigation-shows-televangelists-living-lavish-lifestyles-52662.

12 Harrell, *Oral Roberts: An American Life.*

13 "Millions Sold, No Money Taken: What John Piper Does with His Royalties," at Desiring God website, October 5, 2016. https://www.desiringgod.org/interviews/millions-sold-no-money-taken.

14 Hinn, *God, Greed, and the Prosperity Gospel,* 7-8.

15 Lexico.com, powered by Oxford.

Chapter Fourteen: The Gospel of Self

1 Joel Osteen, *Your Best Life Now: 7 Steps to Living at Your Full Potential* (Nashville: Faith Words, Hachette Book Group, 2014,) 129.

2 Osteen, *Your Best Life Now*, 144.

3 https://largest.org/structures/churches-us/.

4 https://www.joelosteen.com/Pages/AboutJoel.aspx.

5 Osteen, *Your Best Life Now*, 64, 59, 191, 5, 79.

6 Osteen, *Your Best Life Now*, 225, 224.

7 Osteen, *Your Best Life Now*, 249.

8 Osteen, *Your Best Life Now*, 288.

9 Osteen, *Your Best Life Now*, 288.

10 https://www.newsweek.com/president-donald-trump-paula-white-prosperity-gospel-655064?amp=1.

11 https://www.truthforlife.org/resources/sermon/false-faith/.

12 Bill Winston, "Winning the Battle Every Time—Fulfilling Your Dominion Mandate," YouTube.com, Jan. 27, 2018.

13 "The Positivity of Joel Osteen," CBS News, March 27, 2016.

14 https://www.bing.com/videos/search?q=victoria+olstten+we+obey+god+for+ourselves&&view=detail&mid=6083E5B517F-4937392B06083E5B517F4937392B0&&FORM=VRD-GAR&ru=%2Fvideos%2Fsearch%3Fq%3Dvictoria%2Bolstten%2B-we%2Bobey%2Bgod%2Bfor%2Bourselves%26FORM%3DHDRSC3.

15 https://themuslimtimes.info/2019/04/05/joel-osteen-be-comfortable-with-who-you-are/.

16 Evan Plante, Mainsail Ministries, August 5, 2019; http://mainsailm-inistries.org/index.php/q-a-a-god-bible-theology-culture/71-why-is-joel-osteen-considered-a-false-teacher.html.

17 Joel Osteen, *Today's Word*, "Resurrection Power at Work," Apr. 16, 2017; https://www.youtube.com/watch?v=eFrCnA3Py2o

18 https://www.liveinthelight.ca/latest-broadcasts/2019/11/14/happy-are-the-unhappy-p2

19 *The Financial Times*, Edward Luce in Houston, Apr. 18, 2019.

Chapter Fifteen: The Gospel of Rome

1   https://www.breitbart.com/faith/2019/03/06/vatican-catho-

lic-church-membership-worldwide-surpasses-1-3-billion/.

2 *The Catechism of the Catholic Church*, par. 183. Mark 16:16 is used as a proof text.

3 *Catechism*, par. 1814.

4 *Catechism*, par. 1129. This is a restatement of what was originally written in the Catechism of the Council of Trent, 1547, DS 1604.

5 *Catechism*, par. 1113.

6 *Catechism*, par. 1250.

7 *Catechism*, par. 1257.

8 *Catechism*, par. 1213.

9 Catholic.com, Infant Baptism.

10 If you're interested in a better understanding of those difficult passages that touch on both baptism and salvation, I encourage you to visit https://www.gotquestions.org/baptism-salvation.html.

11 *Catechism of the Catholic Church.*, par. 1285.

12 *Catechism*, par. 1302.

13 http://www.aboutcatholics.com/beliefs/catholic-confirmation-explained/

14 https://www.compellingtruth.org/confirmation.html

15 *Catechism of the Catholic Church*, Code of Canon Law, canon 921, sec. 1–2, par. 1389.

16 *Catechism*, par. 1376.

17 *Catechism*, par. 1378.

18 https://www.catholic.org/encyclopedia/view.php?id=9131.

19 *Catechism*, par. 980, Council of Trent, par. 1551: DS 1672; cf. St. Gregory of Nazianzus, Oratio 39, 17: pg. 36, 356.

20 *Catechism*, par. 1441.

21 *Catechism*, par. 1424, compare with par. 1493.

22 *Catechism*, par. 986.

23 *Catechism*, par. 151.

24 *Catechism*, par. 1517.

25 *Catechism*, par. 1532.

26 *Catechism*, par. 1461.

27 *Catechism*, par. 1464.

28 *Catechism*, par. 1470.

29 *Catechism*, par. 1129, par. 2003.

30 Baltimore Catechism lesson 11, question 146.

31 *Catechism of the Catholic Church,* par. 1661.

32 *Catechism*, par. 2068.

33 Council of Trent, Canon 9.

34 *The New St. Joseph Baltimore Catechism*, part 3, The Sacraments and Prayer.

35 Sacerdotalism is defined as "religious belief emphasizing the powers of priests as essential mediators between God and humankind." https://www.merriam-webster.com/dictionary/sacerdotalism https://www.theatlantic.com/international/archive/2018/02/catholic-vatican-china/552800/.

Chapter Sixteen: Light versus Darkness

1 Creighton, Jolene, "How is the Speed of Darkness Faster Than the Speed of Light," August 3, 2014. https://futurism.com/how-is-the-speed-of-darkness-is-faster-than-the-speed-of-light.

Chapter Seventeen: The Mystery of Salvation

1 William MacDonald, *The Gospel of John*, part 1 (Dubuque, Iowa: Emmaus Correspondence School).

2 A. W. Pink, *The Holy Spirit's Work in Salvation* (Pensacola, Florida: Chapel Library).

3 William Haslam, *From Death to Life: Twenty Years of My Ministry* (Brockville, Ontario: Standard Book Room).

Chapter Eighteen: The Wrath of God

1 Keith Getty and Stuart Townend, "In Christ Alone" (London: Kingsway ThankYou Music, 2001). Used by permission.

2 https://www.christiancentury.org/article/2013-04/debating-hymns.

3 http://www.pcusa.org/news/2013/8/9/presbyterian-hymnal-producers-respond-misinformati/.

4 Tertullian, *Against Marcion*, book 1, chap. 27.

5 J. I. Packer, *Knowing God* (Downers Grove, Illinois: IVP Books), p. 151.

6 John MacArthur, "The Final Wrath of God," part 1. https://www.gty.org/.

Chapter Nineteen: The Great Reveal

1 As quoted by Leonardo Blair, "After 40 years, 'megachurch' pastor slams Christianity and quits, deacon claims he had affair," *The Christian Post*, May 7, 2019, https://www.christianpost.com/news/after-40-years-megachurch-pastor-slams-christianity-and-quits-deacon-claims-he-had-affair.html. See also "Fallen Kansas City area pastor leaves wife, family, and the faith," Metro Voice, May 8, 2019. https://metrovoicenews.com/fallen-kansas-city-area-pastor-leaves-wife-familyand-the-faith/.

2 Leonardo Blair, "After 40 years, 'megachurch' pastor slams Christianity and quits, deacon claims he had affair," *The Christian Post*, May 7, 2019, https://www.christianpost.com/news/after-40-years-megachurch-pastor-slams-christianity-and-quits-deacon-claims-he-had-affair.html. See also "Fallen Kansas City area pastor leaves wife, family, and the faith," Metro Voice, May 8, 2019. https://metrovoicenews.com/fallen-kansas-city-area-pastor-leaves-wife-familyand-the-faith/.

3 Jabell1013, Twitter.

4 https://illbehonest.com/charo-washers-testimony-charo-washer, May 20, 2009. See also https://www.bing.com/videos/search?q=examine+yourself+paul+washer+grace&&view=detail&mid=B010227FCD288CDB43F0B010227FCD288CDB43F0&&FORM=VRDGAR.

5 Gary and Mona Shriver, *Unfaithful: Hope and Healing After Infidelity* (Colorado Springs: David C. Cook).

6 Megan Hill, "My Boring Christian Testimony: How I know it's nonetheless real," *Christianity Today,* December 31, 2014. https://www.christianitytoday.com/ct/2014/december/how-i-know-my-testimony-is-real.html

7 John McArthur sermon "Principles of God's Judgment," part 1, gty.org, September 13, 1981.

Chapter Twenty: The Gospel Changes Everything

1 https://www.youtube.com/watch?reload=9&v=hHpTer9Vo0M.

2 Andrew Goud, https://wusuraambya.wordpress.com/.

3 http://www.americandialect.org/Words_of_the_Year_2005.pdf.

Chapter Twenty-One: Nothing but the Truth

1 https://www.lexico.com/definition/post-truth.

2 Stephen Colbert, "The Colbert Report, October 17, 2005; http://www.cc.com/video-clips/63ite2/the-colbert-report-the-word---truthiness.

3 Colin Smith, "Where Grace and Justice Meet," *Life Keys Daily*, September 20, 2018.

4 Lynda Mugglestone, "A journey through spin," OUPblog, September 12, 2011. https://blog.oup.com/2011/09/spin/

5 Dietrich Bonhoeffer, *The Cost of Discipleship* (New York: Touchstone, 1995).

6 Justin Martyr, *First Apology*, quoted in Peter C. Phan, *Social Thought*, vol. 20 of *Message of the Fathers of the Church*, ed. Thomas Halton (Wilmington: Michael Glazier, 1984), 56.

7 Jonathan Morrow, "Are People Free to Believe Whatever They Want About God?" blogpost, August 13, 2014. https://www.jonathanmorrow.org/are-people-free-to-believe-whatever-they-want-about-god/.

Afterword: "Flee from the Wrath to Come"

1 Christian History, Issue 29, 1991, https://www.spurgeongems.org/vols46-48/chs2704.pdf (updated and revised, used with permission). The complete sixty-three volume set of Spurgeon's sermons, as well as other Spurgeon resources, can be accessed at www.spurgeongems.org.

Printed in Great Britain
by Amazon

57398485R00154